Very Short Introductions available now:

For more information visit our websites
www.oup.co.uk/general/vsi/
www.oup.com/us

Jussi M. Hanhimäki

THE UNITED NATIONS

A Very Short Introduction

OXFORD
UNIVERSITY PRESS

OXFORD
UNIVERSITY PRESS

Oxford University Press, Inc., publishes works that further
Oxford University's objective of excellence
in research, scholarship, and education.

Oxford New York
Auckland Cape Town Dar es Salaam Hong Kong Karachi
Kuala Lumpur Madrid Melbourne Mexico City Nairobi
New Delhi Shanghai Taipei Toronto

With offices in
Argentina Austria Brazil Chile Czech Republic France Greece
Guatemala Hungary Italy Japan Poland Portugal Singapore
South Korea Switzerland Thailand Turkey Ukraine Vietnam

Copyright © 2008 by Jussi M. Hanhimäki

Published by Oxford University Press, Inc.
198 Madison Avenue, New York, NY 10016

www.oup.com

Oxford is a registered trademark of Oxford University Press

Library of Congress Cataloging-in-Publication Data
Hanhimäki, Jussi M., 1965–
The United Nations: a very short introduction / Jussi M. Hanhimäki.
p. cm.
Includes bibliographical references and index.
ISBN 978-0-19-530437-4
1. United Nations. I. Title.
JZ4984.5.H364 2008
341.23—dc22
2008018818

3 5 7 9 8 6 4 2

Printed in Great Britain by
Ashford Colour Press Ltd, Gosport, Hants
on acid-free paper

Contents

List of Illustrations

Acknowledgments

I would like to acknowledge the encouragement of my colleagues at the Graduate Institute of International and Development Studies in Geneva, Switzerland, for providing a stimulating environment in which to explore the ins and outs of the United Nations.

At Oxford University Press, I was extremely fortunate to be able to work with an excellent team that, at various points, included Joellyn Ausanka, Tim Bartlett, Mary Sutherland, Justin Tackett, and, in particular, Nancy Toff.

As always my family in Finland has been supportive. Thanks especially to my parents, Hilkka Uuskallio and Jussi K. Hanhimäki, who have never ceased to be supportive. In Geneva, my son, Jari, has allowed his dad to spend hours preparing this book while other pressing matters—tennis, football, trips to aqua park, etc.—would clearly have been far more appropriate ways of using time. Last, I would like to thank Barbara, who insisted that I had to complete this book. While seeing it in print may not change my life, she surely has.

Introduction

We the Peoples: The Promise of the United Nations

"We the peoples of the United Nations," begins the United Nations Charter. It goes on to list four principal aims for the global organization. First, the UN was to safeguard peace and security in order "to save succeeding generations from the scourge of war." Second, it was "to reaffirm faith in fundamental human rights." Third, the UN was to uphold respect for international law. And fourth, the new organization pledged "to promote social progress and better standards of life." In the summer of 1945, the founders of the United Nations thus vowed to make the world a better place.

Has the UN been able to achieve all manner or any of these worthy goals over more than six decades of existence? This is the major question tackled in this book. Accordingly, it will assess the successes and failures of the United Nations as a guardian of international peace and security, as a promoter of human rights, as a protector of international law, and as an engineer of socioeconomic advancement. In doing so, the book will delve into the structure of the UN and its operations throughout the world.

This is not an easy task, for throughout its history the UN has been a controversial institution. Admired by many and reviled by others, the world's only truly global international organization has had a bumpy ride. It has received Nobel Peace Prizes and other awards for saving lives and easing suffering. But it has also been a favorite

1. UN Headquarters, covering eighteen acres on the east side of
Manhattan, consists of four main buildings: the General Assembly
(with sloping roof), the Conference Building (on the East River), the
thirty-nine-floor Secretariat, and the Dag Hammarskjöld Library,
which was added in 1961. The complex was designed by an
international team of eleven architects.

target of politicians who suspect—or claim they do in order to
curry favor with certain groups of voters—the UN of trying to
become a global government. Yet others, such as Henry Cabot
Lodge Jr., the U.S. ambassador to the UN from 1953 to 1960, have
taken a more sober view, recognizing the inherent limits of an
organization that, in theory at least, represents the interests of the
entire world. As Lodge succinctly put it in 1954: "This organization
is created to prevent you from going to hell. It isn't created to
take you to heaven."[1]

Indeed, if there is one theme running through this book it is the simple fact that the UN's greatest challenge has been an impossibly wide gap between its ambitions and capacities. A quick look at the key areas of UN activities should make the case evident.

First, the founders of the UN pledged to make the world a safer place. In order to avoid the sort of carnage caused by World War II, they created a structure and instruments designed to address threats to international security. Most obviously, the UN Security Council was awarded almost limitless power when it came to dealing with violations of peace. Its resolutions were to be binding on all member states. Its underling, the Military Staff Committee, was to plan military operations and have at its disposal an air force contingent ready for immediate deployment. Never again, the founders seem to have hoped, would the world stand by and watch as aggressors violated international borders and agreements.

The design was flawed. The Military Staff Committee did not get its air force or the bases envisioned. Thus, UN military operations could not be deployed rapidly; indeed, the UN was not to have a military arm of its own. The UN charter also contained in it the seeds of the Security Council's immobilization: by granting the veto right to five countries (China, France, Great Britain, the Soviet Union, and the United States), the charter allowed this select group to prevent action that they viewed as being antithetical to their national interests. As a result, the UN may have had a positive role in preventing the outbreak of another world war, but it could not prevent or stop a series of regional conflicts (from Korea and Vietnam to the Middle East and Africa). The peacekeepers sent to the world's trouble regions tended to arrive long after the worst hostilities had ended. Sometimes, as in Sudan's Darfur region after 2003, their arrival was delayed while genocide progressed.

The basic problem for the UN as the overseer of international security was and remains simple: how to deal with conflicts—be they between or within states—without offending the national sovereignty of its member states. It is a riddle that continues to affect the UN's international security functions. Peace is still waiting to break out.

The UN's second goal was to highlight the importance of human rights and respect for international law. To accomplish this objective, treaties, declarations, and legal instruments multiplied. The most important of these documents was undoubtedly the 1948 Universal Declaration of Human Rights. Others were added to the human rights canon in the 1960s, thus producing the International Bill of Rights. By the twenty-first century, the Human Rights Council, the High Commissioner for Human Rights, and other bodies were busily reporting abuses around the world, while the International Criminal Court and special tribunals were prosecuting the worst human rights abusers at The Hague.

But the capacity of these bodies to implement some form of universal jurisdiction remains limited by the very same factor that hampers the UN's role in international security: the prerogative of the nation state. The High Commissioner and the Council cannot give "orders" to sovereign states. The special rapporteurs who investigate abuses on behalf of the international community have to be "invited" by the host government that, in many cases, is the very same government that is being investigated. All too often deadlock has been the end result.

Finally, the UN pledged to promote social and economic progress. To accomplish this, such institutions as the World Bank—linked to but not technically part of the UN system—were set up to assist countries in need of assistance. By the 1960s, as the UN's membership was rising with the proliferation of newly independent and often underdeveloped countries (mainly from Africa), the organization responded by creating additional structures, of which the UN Conference on Trade and Development (UNCTAD) and the UN Development Program (UNDP) are probably the best known.

Two problems, still evident today, emerged as early as the 1960s. On the one hand, there was no agreement on how to promote progress. Economists and social scientists argued over the desirability of giving economic aid as opposed to allowing the market to take care of the work. On the other hand, the different organizations had different resource bases and organizational structures. For example, because the World Bank has been funded mainly by the United States, its policies have been heavily influenced by Washington. But the United States was, for more than four decades, engaged in fighting the Cold War and promoting capitalism over communism as the correct way to organize economic life. In that context, development aid often, too often, became a political tool unrelated to the real problems of real people in the developing world.

Add to this a number of other elements—corruption, interagency competition, and lack of resources—and the reasons why development aid has not been a resounding success become clearer. But neither has it been a complete failure as some of its detractors would have it. Indeed, the so-called Millennium Development Goals (MDGs) unveiled in 2000 called for halving global poverty rates by 2015. By July 7, 2007—the UN's official halfway point for meeting this target—it seemed that Asian countries were on track toward meeting this goal. But sub-Saharan Africa was lagging far behind its targets. It is no accident that the current UN Secretary-General, Ban Ki-moon, has followed in his successors' footsteps in calling for the rich countries to get serious about development aid.

The United Nations may not have lived up to all the ambitions of its founders, yet one fact remains clear: it is the only truly global organization in the history of mankind. With 192 member states as of 2008, the UN covers the entire globe. In its six decades of existence it has almost quadrupled its original membership of 51. The meetings of the UN General Assembly, the forum where all member states are represented, are a true gathering of the proverbial "family of nations" or "the parliament of man."

What lies behind the founding of such a seemingly all-encompassing and potentially all-powerful global organization? Why did its membership increase so dramatically? Why, despite much criticism, does it continue its work around the globe? And what does that work actually involve?

This short book is an attempt to find some answers to these questions, many of them puzzling and frustrating. At the core of my interest, though, is an attempt to explain—both to myself and the readers of this book—the dichotomy that has bothered me ever since I moved to Geneva, the city that is both the original seat of the League of Nations and the current host of the UN's European headquarters.

On the one hand, many of us think of the UN as a bizarre bureaucracy filled with highly (over)paid international civil servants with little else to do with their time but hold conferences in nice cities (such as Geneva) located far away from the world's trouble zones. And yet, on the other hand, we also seem to be of the opinion that the UN helps millions of people around the globe to live better lives or, in many cases, to just hang on to life. Making sense of these widely disparate views of the UN and its role in the modern world is the basic reason that I undertook to write this book.

It has not been easy. For one, it has been necessary to make some tough choices. The choices that I made meant that I would not focus on the slew of resolutions that the UN passes annually. Many UN agencies and funds were omitted, not because they are not important but because the limitation of space did not allow me to discuss, say, the work of the World Tourism Organization (the *other* WTO) or the important analyses produced by the World Meteorological Organization (WMO). Rather, I emphasized the different areas that are the heart of the UN's daily work:

6

international security and peacekeeping; economic and human development; and the advocacy of human rights. Some might object to the fact that I have given short shrift to the UN's environmental and global health agenda. I would simply respond that both of these can be viewed as parts of the broad issues just described.

Second, writing a short book about a vast topic is (inherently) difficult for a historian used to dealing and highlighting complexity over simplicity. Readers will undoubtedly make up their own minds whether the effort was successful. But they should be forewarned that one trace of the fact that the author is a historian was impossible to disguise: the book does often veer toward a narration of events around a specific theme rather than a theoretical explanation and analysis of the functions of a given part of the United Nations.

In the end, one cannot write a book about the UN without addressing a basic question: is the UN obsolete and unnecessary? The answer in this book is no. The UN is an indispensable organization that has made the world a better place, as its founders hoped. But it is also a deeply flawed institution, in need of constant reform.

This, it seems, is not a revolutionary argument. Rather, it reflects the views of most people around the globe. As a 2007 global opinion survey indicates, giving the UN additional powers is a popular proposition around the globe (three out of four of those polled supporting the idea of increasing the powers of the UN Security Council to authorize the use of force). This not only reflects the general dissatisfaction over the way in which the UN is often sidelined by strong countries—the 2003 intervention of Iraq being a recent high-profile case. It is also indicative of the continued hopes that most people in most countries place on the United Nations.

That, alone, makes trying to understand the UN in all its manifold complexity a worthy task.

Chapter 1

The best hope of mankind?
A brief history of the UN

We usually think of international organizations as a twentieth-
century phenomenon that started with the establishment of the
League of Nations in 1919. This is, for the most part, true. However,
in the late nineteenth century nations had already established
international organizations for dealing with specific issues. The
foremost among them were the International Telecommunication
Union (ITU), founded in 1865 (originally called the International
Telegraph Union), and the Universal Postal Union, which dates
back to 1874. Today, both of these organizations are part of the
UN system. The International Peace Conference held in The Hague
in 1899 established the Permanent Court of Arbitration, which
started its work in 1902. It was the first medium for settling
international disputes between countries and a predecessor of the
UN's International Court of Justice. The outbreak of World War I
in August 1914 and the carnage that followed, however, showed the
limits of this mechanism. It also signaled the final end of an
international system—the so-called Concert of Europe—that had
saved the old Continent from the scourge of a major war since
Napoleon's adventures a century earlier.

Between 1914 and 1918, Europe saw the worst killing spree of its
already bloody history. Almost twenty million people perished.
Empires (the Ottoman, the Austro-Hungarian, and, temporarily,
the Russian) collapsed. New nations (such as Czechoslovakia,

Estonia, and Finland) were born. Radical revolutions were won (in Russia) and lost (in Germany). In short, a new world order emerged.

The League of Nations: "a definite guaranty of peace"

Amid the carnage, in January 1918, President Woodrow Wilson outlined his idea of the League of Nations. Given the utter devastation caused by World War I, support for the idea of an international organization was widespread. To many, an international organization with the power to settle disputes before they escalated into military conflicts appeared to be the answer. Although the United States would eventually fail to join the League of Nations, Wilson chaired the 1919 Versailles Peace Conference's commission on the establishment of an international organization. Wilson, for one, had few reservations about the significance of the League. As he declared to a joint session of the U.S. Congress in 1919:

> It is a definite guaranty of peace. It is a definite guaranty by word against aggression. It is a definite guaranty against the things which have just come near bringing the whole structure of civilization into ruin. Its purposes do not for a moment lie within. The purposes are declared, and its powers are unmistakable. It is not in contemplation that this should be merely a league to secure the peace of the world. It is a league which can be used for cooperation in any international matter.[1]

The president was not alone in placing such high hopes in the new organization. Wilson, with his open idealism and fresh internationalism, offered a ray of hope for a better future. But in retrospect, Wilson's confident rhetoric appears out of place. The new League was dealt a devastating blow when the U.S. Senate refused to ratify the Versailles Treaty. The country never joined the League, making the newly formed organization permanently handicapped.

2. President Woodrow Wilson rides with French premier Georges Clemenceau to the signing of the Treaty of Versailles.

Nevertheless, after being housed temporarily in London, the League commenced its operations in Geneva, Switzerland, in 1920. It soon scored some limited successes. In the early 1920s, the League settled territorial disputes between Finland and Sweden over the Aland Islands, between Germany and Poland over Upper Silesia, and between Iraq and Turkey over the city of Mosul. The League combated the international opium trade and alleviated refugee crises in Russia with some success. By acting as the umbrella organization for such agencies as the International Labor Organization (ILO) and the Permanent Court of International Justice (predecessor of today's International Court of Justice, ICJ), it also provided a model for the future United Nations.

A victors' organization, the League was dominated by France and Great Britain, with Japan and Italy as the other two permanent members of the League Council (the rough equivalent to the UN Security Council and the highest authority on matters of international security). The twenty-eight founding members, represented in the General Assembly, were mostly from Europe and Latin America.

Indeed, the League of Nations was in this sense an expression of the Eurocentric world of its times: virtually all of Africa, Asia, and the Middle East were controlled by European imperial powers. To be sure, the League established the so-called mandate system to prepare the "natives" of the different regions for self-government and independence. The governments that received the mandates—for example, Britain in Palestine and France in Lebanon and Syria—were granted broad authority regarding such preparations. They took their time. Independence for most European mandates would have to wait until after 1945 and would be accompanied by much violence, instability, and, in the long run, chronic insecurity.

Shortsighted though they were, the mandates were a time bomb that would explode only *after* the League had ceased to exist. It was the League's failure to prevent the outbreak of World War II that caused its demise.

The world at war

Although the absence of the United States was a significant factor in rendering the League of Nations ineffectual, the organization's importance was further minimized by the lack of respect it commanded among other great powers. Germany and the Soviet Union were members, but only briefly: Germany joined in 1926, only to exit the League after the Nazis came to power in 1933. In 1933 the Soviet Union entered the League. Six years later, after its attack on Finland in late 1939, the USSR became the only League member ever to be expelled.

By that point the League had also seen the departure of two of its founding members. Unhappy with the League's criticism of its occupation of Manchuria, Japan left the club in 1933. In 1935–36 Italy was equally dismissive of its membership obligations after its successful attack and occupation of Ethiopia, one of the three African members of the League (the others were Liberia and South Africa).

Why did the League fail in countering this series of aggressive acts by a number of great powers willing to use military force for expansionist purposes? The global economic crisis of the 1930s certainly curbed the enthusiasm of others—France and Britain in particular—to risk lives and resources to fight distant wars that did not have an immediate bearing on their national security. Thus, they turned to appeasement, a policy that ultimately failed. During the 1938 Munich Conference, Britain and France acquiesced in the dismantlement of Czechoslovakia by agreeing to the addition of the Sudetenland to Hitler's Reich. If that act had been justified by the existence of a large German-speaking population in the ceded parts of Czechoslovakia, there might have been no excuse for Germany's later occupation of the remainder of Czechoslovakia. When Germany finally attacked Poland in September 1939, after concluding a sinister pact with the Soviet Union a month earlier, the high hopes placed upon the League only two decades earlier were completely crushed.

The League of Nations was further handicapped by its inability to apply sufficient pressure in clear-cut cases of aggression. According to its covenant, the League could introduce verbal or economic sanctions against an aggressor and, if these methods failed, intervene militarily. In theory these steps were logical and reasonable. But while verbal sanctions could not deter an aggressor that was determined and strong, economic sanctions required international collaboration. As the League had no authority beyond its limited membership, a country suffering from the pressure of economic sanctions could still trade with nonmembers. Especially during the international economic crisis of the 1930s, willing trading partners were not hard to find. Because the League had no army of its own, military intervention required member countries to furnish the necessary troops. In practice this meant French or British troops, but neither country was interested in getting involved in potentially costly conflicts in Africa or Asia.

By the time the League expelled the Soviet Union in 1939, there was no getting around the fact that the League had failed in its overall objective. It had not become, as Wilson had hoped, a "definite guaranty for peace." Nevertheless, the onset of World War II made it even more evident that some form of international organization was needed to safeguard against yet another descent to Armageddon in the future. One goal was paramount: a repetition of the League experience could not be allowed.

An act of creation

The first "Declaration by United Nations" dates back to January 1, 1942, when representatives of twenty-six nations pledged their governments to continue fighting together to defeat the Axis powers and to obtain a "just" peace. Thus, unlike the League, the UN started off as an alliance that came into being soon after the American entry to the war, following the Japanese attack on Pearl Harbor and Germany's declaration of war on the United States in December 1941. World War II became a truly global conflict, pitting the so-called Grand Alliance (headed by the United States, Great Britain, and the Soviet Union) against the Axis powers (Germany, Italy, and Japan).

World War II was, simply, deadly. The estimated civilian and military death tolls ran as high as 72 million. The deeper impact of the war on global and national economies, as well as on political structures around the globe, was profound. European empires collapsed either during or as a result of the war. The United States and the Soviet Union emerged as the strongest nations on earth. Germany and Japan were occupied and militarily emasculated. In sum, the world was transformed.

The UN was created, in part, to manage that transformation. As in the case of the League, it was an initiative of the American president, in this case Franklin D. Roosevelt, whose administration

3. After months of intense negotiations, the UN Charter was officially adopted on June 25, 1945. A member of the Guatemalan delegation signs the charter at the official signing ceremony the next day.

pushed for the creation of the UN during the last years of the war. In August 1944 delegates from China, the Soviet Union, the United Kingdom, and the United States met at Dumbarton Oaks, a private estate in Washington, D.C., to draw up the basic blueprint for the new international organization. By October the outline for the UN Charter was ready. After the surrender of Germany in April of the following year (and the death of Roosevelt in the same month), the charter was signed in San Francisco on June 26, 1945. On October 24, 1945, with the Pacific war also concluded, the United Nations officially came into existence.

The basic issue with which the drafters of the UN Charter dealt was in essence unchanged from the one Wilson and his European counterparts had faced in 1918–19. They wanted to create an organization that would, indeed, be a definite guaranty of peace. There was plenty of skepticism, understandably so given the fate of the League's lofty goals. And, as earlier, the basic dilemmas and conundrums had not changed: How to balance national sovereignty and international idealism? How to reconcile the imbalances between countries over power and influence, over resources and commitments? How, in other words, could one draft a charter that would recognize and effectively deal with the sheer fact that some countries were, in effect, more equal than others? How could one make sure that some countries would not simply walk out—as Japan had done in the 1930s—when it did not like the decisions of the UN?

The men who drafted the UN Charter addressed this issue with a simple mechanism: the veto power. In other words, the charter gave superior powers to five of the founding members of the UN—China, France, Great Britain, the United States, and the USSR—that allowed them to prevent any decisions that they viewed inimical to their interests from being made. They became the Permanent Five (P 5) of the UN Security Council, countries that would have both a seat in the most important body of the new organization as long as it existed. This strategy, it was thought, would provide the key countries with an incentive to remain part of the UN. It also provided them with the means of neutralizing the world organization.

Although its founders were keenly aware of the failures of the League of Nations, most of its ideals and many structural elements were at the core of the UN Charter. Most evidently, the UN Charter and the League Covenant cited the promotion of international security and the peaceful settlement of disputes as key goals. But the UN Charter was different in two important respects.

The UN Charter in brief

The UN Charter consists of a series of articles divided into chapters. Chapter 1 sets forth the general purposes of the United Nations, most importantly the maintenance of international peace and security. Chapter 2 defines the general criteria for membership in the United Nations; it was open to "all peace-loving states." Applicants would, however, have to be "recommended" by the UN Security Council, thus giving the UNSC the right to veto any country's membership.

The bulk of the document is contained in chapters 3 through 15, which describe the organs and institutions of the UN and their respective powers. Perhaps the most important chapters, however, are those dealing with the enforcement powers of the key UN bodies. Chapters 6 and 7, for example, discuss the Security Council's power to investigate and mediate disputes as well as its power to authorize sanctions or the use of military force. Subsequent chapters deal with the UN's powers for economic and social cooperation; the Trusteeship Council, which oversaw decolonization; the powers of the International Court of Justice; and the functions of the United Nations Secretariat, the administrative arm (or permanent bureaucracy) of the UN.

It differed from the League Covenant particularly in its emphasis on the promotion of social and economic progress as a central goal. The latter had been part of the League of Nations Covenant as well, but it appeared, and then only briefly, in article 23. In contrast, the very preamble of the UN Charter reads: "to employ international machinery for the promotion of the economic and social advancement of all peoples."

The reason for highlighting the significance of economic and social development was rooted in the interwar years. Many saw the global economic depression of the late 1920s and 1930s as the root cause of the political upheavals that had led to the rise of ultranationalism and the acts of aggression that had produced World War II. Thus, promoting economic and social equality was seen as a way of safeguarding international security.

The founders of the UN wanted to create an organization that would be able to prevent that "scourge of war" from descending upon mankind yet again. For this purpose, they defined the question of international security in broader terms than had those who erected the League of Nations. They also aimed to create a structure that would allow the UN to be an active participant in world affairs in its key areas: military security, economic and social development, and the upholding of human rights and international justice.

In a sense, there was something for everybody but also a recipe for future conundrums.

The early Cold War and the UN

The original signatories of the UN Charter hardly expected that the simple act of creation would guarantee a peaceful world order. In fact, the UN shared a significant common feature with its predecessor. Like the League of Nations, the UN was, at its very founding, a "victors' organization." Major wartime adversaries and their allies and co-belligerents were not awarded membership until later. For example, the first UN Security Council members included Brazil, Egypt, Mexico, New Zealand, Norway, and Poland; Italy, Japan and Germany were left out. Nevertheless, the hope that the UN would be a more effective force in safeguarding international security rested on the fact that its founders did include both the United States and the Soviet Union.

As the delegates of fifty-one nations arrived for the first series of meetings in London in January 1946, the general atmosphere of international relations was already deteriorating. In February, Soviet leader Joseph Stalin made a much criticized speech in which he described a world irrevocably divided between two economic and political systems. On March 5, 1946, former British prime minister Winston Churchill responded by declaring that an Iron Curtain had descended across Europe. A year later, the U.S. president Harry Truman unveiled the Truman Doctrine, the first public expression of America's long-term strategy of containing the expansion of Soviet and communist influence.

Subsequent descent to the Cold War was rapid. By February 1948 the establishment of the Iron Curtain in East-Central Europe was concluded when Czechoslovakia joined the ranks of Soviet bloc communist dictatorships. In Western Europe, the United States assumed a preponderant position as the counterweight to Soviet influence by assisting the anticommunist faction in the Greek Civil War, offering aid to Turkey because that country was being pressed by the USSR and, most significantly, launching the European Recovery Program, which, between 1948 and 1952, boosted the economic recovery of Western Europe. The creation of the North Atlantic Treaty Organization (NATO) in April 1949 cemented the division of Europe into two hostile blocs. In subsequent years (and decades) the Cold War became increasingly global and militarized. The creation of the People's Republic of China on October 1, 1949, was quickly followed by the Sino-Soviet alliance and, in June 1950, the outbreak of the Korean War, which presented the UN with its first severe challenge.

The onset of the Cold War and the outbreak of the first major hot war of the post-1945 era did not destroy the UN. But it did fundamentally shape its role in international relations and restricted its ability to act as a positive force for international security. The Korean conflict was to remain the only large-scale UN military intervention during the Cold War era, made possible only by the absence of the USSR from the Security Council sessions in June 1950; the Soviets were boycotting the UN's refusal to admit the newly constituted People's Republic of China into the organization. Thus, the Soviet representative was not there to

18

veto a resolution sponsored by the United States, a right that the USSR employed no fewer than eighty times between 1946 and 1955.

The Soviet use of the veto was, in fact, linked to another Cold War–induced handicap: the deadlock in adding new members to the UN. Being a "peace-loving state" clearly did not suffice as a qualification. During the first decade after San Francisco only nine countries were added to the roster: Afghanistan, Iceland, Sweden, and Thailand in 1946; Pakistan and Yemen in 1947; Burma (now Myanmar) in 1948; Israel in 1949; and Indonesia in 1950. How much more "peace-loving" some of these countries were when compared to such persistent applicants as Finland or Austria is questionable.

In fact, there was no shortage of applicants. But the Korean War (1950–53) made any cooperation between the United States and the Soviet Union virtually impossible. On top of this there was a Soviet-American disagreement over procedure: while the Soviets wanted a package deal that would ensure the simultaneous addition of roughly an equal number of pro-Soviet, pro-American, and neutral states to the UN roster, the United States insisted that each application should be decided upon the merits of the specific country. The end result was a deadlock: after 1950 no new members were added for five years.

Most of all, however, the controversy over the People's Republic of China's (PRC) bid to join the UN and the Security Council severely hurt the organization's credibility in the 1950s and 1960s. Having won the Chinese civil war in 1949, the PRC—or "Red China" as most American politicians called it—claimed that it was the rightful representative of *all* Chinese. This notion was vehemently rejected by the Republic of China (ROC, or Taiwan), which, as an ally of the United States, received constant American support. For more than two decades Taiwan—a small island off the Chinese coast where the Nationalist Chinese had fled after communist victory—represented China in the UN. Most crucially, Taiwan wielded a veto right in the Security Council as though it was one of the world's five great powers. Only in 1971, when the Nixon administration wished to open a diplomatic relationship to the PRC, did Washington change its policy of nonrecognition of the PRC. Beijing, however, remained adamant in its claim to represent all of China. Thus, the PRC replaced Taiwan in the UN and the Security Council, leaving the island and its population of approximately 22 million outside the UN.

Although the emergence of the Cold War fundamentally affected the UN's effectiveness in its first decade, there were a number of positive developments as well. None of these was more significant than the 1948 adoption of the Universal Declaration of Human Rights, a document negotiated under the leadership of Eleanor Roosevelt, widow of the former president. Also in 1948, the UN sent its first peace observers to South Asia and the Middle East. In the latter region, the civil rights activist Ralph Bunche successfully mediated armistice agreements between the new state of Israel and its Arab neighbors in 1948–49. In the same period, the UN was active in dealing with the needs of World War II European refugees, resulting ultimately in the creation of the office of the UN High Commissioner for Refugees (UNHCR) in 1950.

But such milestones could not mask the fact that during its first decade the UN was hostage to a highly charged international climate. In particular, only a shift in the nature of the Cold War could resolve the membership deadlock that by the mid-1950s began to undermine the UN's credibility as a truly open international organization.

Decolonization and development

Sixteen countries joined the UN in 1955, bringing the total number of members to seventy-six. The sudden enlargement came as a result of a package deal in which Eastern members such as

Albania, Bulgaria, and Hungary were balanced against such Western ones as Italy, Portugal, and Spain. In addition, the package deal included a number of neutral European countries (Austria, Finland, and Ireland) and a few that had been recently granted independence (Cambodia, Laos, and Libya).

The 1955 package deal reflected a temporary easing of East-West tensions in the aftermath of Stalin's death and the end of the Korean War. Only a year later, however, international tensions again increased as two virtually simultaneous crises erupted. In October 1956, Soviet troops intervened to crush a democracy movement in Hungary. The brutal suppression did not lead to any American action—in part because it coincided with an ill-fated British, French, and Israeli attack on Egypt after Egyptian leader Gamal Abdel Nasser had announced the nationalization of the Suez Canal. Ironically, the Suez crisis prompted the first significant case in which the Americans and Soviets found themselves on the same side at the UN: both voted in favor of a resolution calling for the immediate withdrawal of foreign troops from Egypt.

The 1956 Suez crisis is sometimes described as a moment that crystallized the end of European imperial pretensions. In the years that followed, the bulk of the Belgian, British, and French colonies gained independence. As they did so, the new nations worked hard to gain rapid international recognition. One of the most important symbols of their new nationhood was membership in the UN.

It is therefore not surprising that the number of countries added to the UN in 1955 soon paled when compared to the expansion that followed. Between 1956 and 1968 the membership grew to 119 (by 1962 the UN had already doubled its original roster of fifty-one). With a few exceptions (Japan, which joined in 1956, the foremost among them), these new members consisted of former African and Asian colonies of European powers. Most were economically

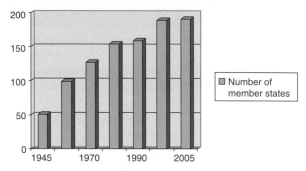

CHART 1.1 **The growth of UN membership since 1945.**

backward when compared to the original members. In the twenty-first century many continue to be wrecked by civil conflicts and have become permanent theaters of various UN operations.

The new nations had another common feature: the bulk of them refused to choose a side in the East-West confrontation, opting for membership in the so-called Nonaligned Movement (NAM) instead. The movement started out with a meeting of twenty-five nations at Belgrade, Yugoslavia, in 1961. In subsequent decades NAM grew to a grouping of more than one hundred nations that transcended the Cold War. In 2006, for example, it held another summit meeting in Havana, Cuba. NAM has been, since the 1970s, the largest grouping of countries represented in the UN General Assembly.

The main impact of NAM was to place the focus of UN activities and concerns on social and economic questions, particularly on the unequal distribution of wealth between the countries of the global North and South. The first UN Conference on Trade and Development (UNCTAD), held in 1964, highlighted this goal by the formation of the Group of 77 (G-77), a loose organization of developing countries in Latin America, Asia, and Africa that attempts to keep development aid at the center of the UN's agenda.

In this they have been successful. The expanded UN clearly honed in on economic, social, and environmental questions in the 1960s and 1970s. There were major UN-sponsored international conferences on the environment (1972) and the status of women (1975). The UN adopted conventions against racial discrimination (1969) and to combat gender-based intolerance and discrimination (1979). And the UN Environment Programme (UNEP) succeeded in pushing for the signing of the Treaty on the Protection of the Ozone Layer (the Montreal Protocol) in 1987. In 1980 the World Health Organization (WHO) declared smallpox extinct (the last case having been reported in 1977). While the organization's ability to deal with international security issues (particularly with interstate and intrastate wars) was in some doubt throughout the Cold War, the UN was actively addressing the many other global challenges, particularly those facing its newer member states.

The UN in the post–Cold War era

The collapse of the Soviet Union and the end of the Cold War transformed international politics and the UN. With the disappearance of the persistent East-West confrontation, many expected that the UN Security Council would finally take its rightful role as the provider and guarantor of international peace and security. According to the "Agenda for Peace," adopted in the summer of 1992, the UN would use preventive diplomacy, peacemaking, and peacekeeping to make its mark on the post–Cold War international order. With the superpower confrontation over, development aid was supposed to become less politicized. Hence, in 1994 the UN published its "Agenda for Development." Not to be outdone, human rights activists pushed through an "Agenda for Democracy" in 1996. If the number of agendas was to be any guide, a golden age of global governance was at hand. "This era of global challenges leaves no choice but cooperation at the global level," maintained UN Secretary-General Kofi Annan upon receiving the Nobel Peace Prize in 2001.[2]

Annan, the charming Ghanaian who led the UN for a decade (1997–2007), was undoubtedly right. But he surely knew that his high-minded ideals were far from being realized at the start of the new millennium. The decade and a half after the end of the Cold War has seen many changes both in the UN's policies and within the organization itself. But greater relevance in determining global affairs is hardly among them.

There has been growth in numerous ways. UN membership has increased from 159 countries in 1989 to 192 in 2007. In the same period the UN budget jumped from $2.6 billion to roughly $20 billion. This has resulted partly from the increase in the number of UN peace operations since the end of the Cold War. Thirteen operations were undertaken in the first four decades of the UN's existence; thirty-six have been authorized since 1988. In 2007 there were approximately 80,000 UN peacekeepers around the globe, compared to 13,000 two decades earlier. The cost of these operations grew tenfold: from approximately $500 million in the late 1980s to $5 billion in 2006. At the same time the UN was almost hyperactive in its presentation of numerous ambitious undertakings and plans, prompted by countless studies and conferences. Much of this activism was crystallized in 2000, when the UN unveiled its Millennium Development Program: a list of eight universal goals that ranged from halving extreme poverty to halting the spread of HIV/AIDS and providing universal primary education. This was all to be achieved by 2015.

Such growth and activism could not, however, mask the harsh realities that the UN faced in the post–Cold War era. Despite the explosion in the number of its peace operations, the balance between success and failure tended to tilt toward the latter. Although the UN may have succeeded in the transformation of Namibia to majority rule, for example, it failed in preventing massive killings in former Yugoslavia or Rwanda. Though the percentage of people living in extreme poverty in Asia may have declined in the early years of the twenty-first century, similar numbers had gone up in Africa.

The UN's first six decades were, thus, replete with change. The growth in membership alone meant that the organization was, by the early twenty-first century, the only truly global institution. But this development was filled with challenges and frustrations as the rapidly transforming UN dealt with, among others, questions of international and human security, post-conflict management, human rights, and social and economic development. Operating on a global scale, with an international staff and within the overall context of a conflict-ridden international system, the UN usually had only mixed success in any of these fields.

One clue to understanding why this is the case lies within the hybrid structure of the international organization itself.

Chapter 2

An impossible hybrid: the structure of the United Nations

In an interview with *Time* magazine in the summer of 1955, Dag Hammarskjöld expressed his frustration over the UN's public image. He worried, in particular, that many people considered the organization—at the time barely ten years old—as a bureaucratic monstrosity incapable of addressing the real concerns of real people. Equally important, Hammarskjöld thought that such disaffection was distancing the UN from the very people it was designed to serve. There was but one solution. As Hammarskjöld explained: "Everything will be all right—you know when? When people, just people, stop thinking of the United Nations as a weird Picasso abstraction and see it as a drawing they made themselves."[1]

The second UN Secretary-General's remarks are indicative of one of the central problems of the world organization. In 1955 the UN was indeed present but distant, not the least because the UN worked in so many different fields, through so many different agencies, and with such a variety of different goals. It was, as it still remains, "a weird Picasso abstraction," an organizational hybrid, its many functions impossible to explain in plain language. There is no point in mincing words: the UN is a structural monstrosity, a conglomeration of organizations, divisions, bodies, and secretariats all with their distinctive acronyms that few can ever imagine being able to master. This, alone, explains many of the UN's problems.

The central point, though, is that the rationale behind the creation of this hybrid—the Picasso abstraction in Hammarskjöld's words—is simple: it was made up by people from many nations, with divergent backgrounds and goals. Equally important, the founders of the UN (and the designers of its structure) were faced with the everlasting dilemma: how to reconcile national interests—national security, national prosperity, national laws—with the international—international security, global development, universal justice, and human rights. The structure that was created reflected this dilemma and is one of the reasons for the outcome: a painting that is part abstraction, part real.

The UN "family"

In 1945 the six principal organs of the UN were the General Assembly, Security Council, Economic and Social Council, Trusteeship Council, International Court of Justice, and the Secretariat. With the exception of the Trusteeship Council, which became obsolete with the completion of the decolonization process it oversaw, these organs still constitute the basic superstructure of the UN. All of them meet regularly, and their members vote and make decisions, issue declarations, and debate the issues of the day. Yet the functions of these organs are vastly different: while the GA is basically the parliament of the UN and the Security Council its executive committee, the Secretariat is the operational body of—or the bureaucracy that runs—the UN.

The UN "family," though, is much larger, encompassing fifteen agencies and several programs and bodies. Some of the organizations, such as the International Labor Organization (ILO), were founded during the League of Nations era in the 1920s. Many more have been created since 1945 to address the specific problems that the UN has been called to solve. Much of this proliferation—and the ensuing complexity of the UN—is the result of a rapid growth in membership that, in the decades following the founding of the organization, contributed to the

The United Nations system

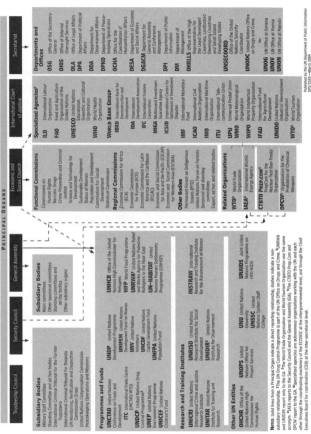

CHART 2.1 The United Nations System

escalation of the tasks that the UN has been charged to undertake. As a result, new bodies and programs have been (and continue to be) added on a regular basis. Others, such as the United Nations High Commissioner for Refugees (UNHCR), were originally meant to be temporary but have since been transformed into permanent organs. Some, inevitably, overlap with others.

To top it all off, the UN has a hybrid set of "subsidiaries" and partners. Throughout its history, the UN has associated with almost three thousand NGOs. This was already envisioned in 1945: article 77 of the UN Charter explicitly states that the UN "may make suitable arrangements for consultation with non-governmental organizations [NGOs] which are concerned with matters within its competence." In practice this means that every year the UN works together with hundreds of NGOs to undertake humanitarian tasks in the world's conflict zones. For example, between 1995 and 2002 the UN Mission in Bosnia and Herzegovina (UNMIBH) oversaw that country's process of peacebuilding—most significantly the establishment of the rule of law—after a nasty war. Throughout the period it participated with close to forty local NGOs that offered their expertise on a wide range of competencies ranging from the clearing of land mines to protecting the environment.

In addition to their cooperation with the many UN missions, NGOs also act as lobbying groups for various causes. In 2007, for example, thirty-two NGOs issued an open letter "urging" UN Secretary-General Ban Ki-moon to pressure Sudan's reluctant government into permitting a Joint African Union/United Nations Peacekeeping Force to enter the conflict-ridden Darfur region. This example hints at another way in which the UN has increasingly been forced to admit the limits of its own capacities and forge alliances elsewhere. Particularly since the early 1990s, the UN has "subcontracted" peacekeeping tasks to non-UN institutions (such regional organizations as NATO or the African Union) or even to private security companies. In 2001 the latter even formed their own NGO, the International Peace Operations Association (IPOA), which acts as a public relations lobbying group for firms that in previous times would have been referred to as bands of mercenaries.

This structural complexity also reflects an effort to create an organization that would avoid some of the problems faced by the League of Nations and one that could adapt to the changing international environment as needed. The League had had as many similar organs as the UN. For example, there had been the League Council (an executive committee that resembled the UN Security Council) and the League Assembly (the rough equivalent of the UN General Assembly). The UN's organization was ultimately based on a combination of inherited structures, new challenges, and historical lessons.

The Security Council

The Security Council is the central organ of the entire UN system. It has primary responsibility for the maintenance of international peace and security. To that effect, the SC was granted wide powers that would make it an active participant in international affairs. It could investigate any dispute or situation that might lead to international friction and it was authorized to decide on economic sanctions or military action. The SC was therefore mandated to use its powers both as a means of preventing a conflict and as a way of enforcing a state's compliance with a specific decision or resolution.

The wide powers granted to the Security Council can be understood as a result of the desire to build a more effective guardian of international peace and security than the League of Nations had been. Few at the time or afterwards have disputed the need for such an organization. But the structure of the SC is not unproblematic. It reflects one of the central tensions that have overshadowed the UN—and often hampered its

Chapter 7 of the UN Charter defines the Security Council's prerogatives. Some of the key articles include:

Article 39

The Security Council shall determine the existence of any threat to the peace, breach of the peace, or act of aggression and shall make recommendations, or decide what measures shall be taken in accordance with Articles 41 and 42, to maintain or restore international peace and security.

Article 40

In order to prevent an aggravation of the situation, the Security Council may, before making the recommendations or deciding upon the measures provided for in Article 39, call upon the parties concerned to comply with such provisional measures as it deems necessary or desirable. Such provisional measures shall be without prejudice to the rights, claims, or position of the parties concerned. The Security Council shall duly take account of failure to comply with such provisional measures.

Article 41

The Security Council may decide what measures not involving the use of armed force are to be employed to give effect to its decisions, and it may call upon the Members of the United Nations to apply such measures. These may include complete or partial interruption of economic relations and of rail, sea, air, postal, telegraphic, radio, and other means of communication, and the severance of diplomatic relations.

Article 42

Should the Security Council consider that measures provided for in Article 41 would be inadequate or have proved to be

(Continued)

Chapter 7 of the UN Charter   (continued)

inadequate, it may take such action by air, sea, or land forces as may be necessary to maintain or restore international peace and security. Such action may include demonstrations, blockade, and other operations by air, sea, or land forces of Members of the United Nations.

Article 43

1. All Members of the United Nations, in order to contribute to the maintenance of international peace and security, undertake to make available to the Security Council, on its call and in accordance with a special agreement or agreements, armed forces, assistance, and facilities, including rights of passage, necessary for the purpose of maintaining international peace and security....

effectiveness. In particular, its two-tiered membership organization, which gave disproportionately more power to five of the major victorious powers of World War II, recognized Great Power prerogatives as an important element of the UN Charter. The nation-state and narrow national interests were thus juxtaposed against the universal ideals that were at the foundation of the UN.

The Security Council was initially made up of eleven members (or states), a number that was increased to fifteen in 1965. Of these, five—the United States, Great Britain, France, China, and Russia (until 1991 the Soviet Union)—are permanent members (known as the P-5). The other ten are nonpermanent members, elected by the UN General Assembly for two-year terms. Their selection reflects an effort to find some—but hardly perfect—regional balance: Africa has three seats, while Western Europe and Oceania, Asia, and Latin America and the Caribbean each get two. The last seat is reserved for Eastern Europe. Each year five of these ten nonpermanent members leave the SC and are replaced.

Two key features differentiate the Security Council from the League Council. First, the decisions of the Security Council are binding and require a majority of nine out of fifteen—rather than unanimity as was the case in the League—to be passed. Second, the permanent members are clearly more powerful than the nonpermanent ones: any one of the five can block a decision by using its right of veto. This clause has prompted numerous calls for reform: the five permanent members may have been the "great powers" of 1945; they certainly were the key victorious powers of World War II. This is not automatically the case in the twenty-first century, though. But since the founding of the UN the only major reform has been the increase in the number of nonpermanent members in 1965.

The concentration of power in the hands of five countries has been a subject of criticism in large part because the SC exercises a broad range of powers over the rest of the UN system. For example, the SC can recommend the admission of new member states, it basically chooses the Secretary-General, and, with the GA, it selects the judges of the International Court of Justice.

Faulty or not, the Security Council and its five permanent members simply overshadow all other organs of the UN.

The General Assembly

If the UNSC is where the UN—or those countries that are members of the SC at any given time—usually reacts to the many conflicts around the globe, the General Assembly (GA) is the forum where each of the 192 member states can make its case heard. As the main deliberative organ of the United Nations, it is in many ways akin to a national parliament. Each member state, regardless of its size, has one vote. This arrangement seems to make the GA much like the U.S. Senate, where each of the fifty states is

4. Nikita Khrushchev, premier of the USSR, at a meeting of the UN General Assembly in September 1960. His visit to the UN is best remembered for the day the fiery Soviet leader banged his shoe on the lectern to reinforce his oratory.

represented by two senators regardless of the size of the population or landmass of a given state. The situation is in some ways absurd: the tiny island of Tuvalu with its 11,600 citizens has equal representation with the People's Republic of China and India, each with more than 1 billion.

The very size of the GA means that its effectiveness is limited. The annual meetings—or regular sessions—that usually open in September have become ritualistic and tend to make news only in connection with a possible high-profile appearance, by the U.S. president, for instance. Indeed, the UNGA has acquired perhaps its most obvious significance as a protest forum for disaffected would-be nations (such as the Palestinians since 1970s).

Its very inclusiveness is the GA's—and in a nutshell the UN's—greatest weakness: with so many members represented, contentious issues have little chance of being affirmatively decided. This is particularly so because decisions on key questions—on peace and security, admission of new members, and budgetary matters—require a two-thirds majority (decisions on other questions are by simple majority). On questions of international security the GA is ultimately subservient to the Security Council and, hence, dependent on consensus among the P-5.

In many ways, the General Assembly functions like a national parliament. It has a president and twenty-one (!) vice presidents. Unlike most national parliaments with their political parties, however, the GA is divided along regional lines. The presidency, for example, rotates each year among five groups of states: African, Asian, Eastern European, Latin American and the Caribbean, and Western European and other states (for example, the United States, Canada, Australia, and New Zealand).

In addition, the GA's work is carried out in a number of committees with a more limited membership. These are charged with dealing with such specific issues as Disarmament and International Security (first main committee); Economic and Financial questions (second); and Social, Humanitarian and Cultural issues (third). As in the case of the presidency and vice presidency, the membership and chairmanships of the committees is selected on a regional basis. For example, in 2006 the first committee was chaired by a Norwegian, the second by an Estonian, the third by an Iraqi, the fourth by a Nepalese, and so on.

If the SC has remained remarkably static in terms of its rules and membership, the GA is the UN body where the gradual proliferation of member countries—from 51 in 1945 to 192 today—has been most visible. This explosion of membership has affected the UN in a number of important ways, the most important one probably being the crystallization of economic and social development as the key issues on the UN's agenda. It has also affected the work of those who run the organization on a daily basis.

Secretary-General: "the most difficult job on earth"?

The UN Secretariat serves the other principal organs of the United Nations and administers the programs and policies laid down by them. At its head is the Secretary-General, who is appointed by the General Assembly on the recommendation of the Security Council for a renewable five-year term. The entire secretariat consists of approximately 9,000 international civil servants working at UN duty stations around the world (mainly in Addis Ababa, Bangkok, Beirut, Geneva, Nairobi, New York, Santiago, and Vienna).

The role of the Secretariat is multifaceted, ranging from public advocacy of various UN causes and the day-to-day administration of its various economic and social programs to crisis diplomacy and overseeing the work of UN peacekeeping forces in the trouble spots of the world. Balancing these tasks while under pressure from the member states has never been easy for this relatively small body of international civil servants who are, after all, citizens of the member states. The work of the Secretariat is, by the sheer composition of the personnel, under constant pressure from the

5. At the airport in Salisbury, Southern Rhodesia, an honor guard escorts Dag Hammarskjöld's body onto a plane for the journey to his hometown in Sweden. Hammarskjöld was killed in a plane crash in 1961 while trying to resolve a crisis in the Congo.

dyad of nation-state imperatives and universal goals. Can one truly expect that a national of a given country will not use his or her position as a UN functionary to push certain policies that would have a positive impact on his or her native country?

This point has clearly affected the makeup of the Secretariat and the selection of the UN Secretary-General (UNSG). Since 1946 the UNSG has been the public face—as well as the chief administrative officer—of the organization. The post of the UNSG combines enormous visibility and expectations with limited powers. Ideally independent from national prerogatives and above politics, the UNSG and the Secretariat as a whole cannot function without the support of the constituent nation-states, most specifically the five permanent members of the Security Council. Because the physical headquarters of the UN are in New York, the UNSG is particularly open to the scrutiny of the American media, making him a subject of partisan wrangling—as well as criticism and disdain—within the most powerful nation-state in the world.

The first UNSG, the Norwegian Trygve Lie, summed up the difficulties of the post when passing the job to the Swede Dag Hammarskjöld in 1953: "Welcome to the most difficult job on earth." Earlier, Lie—who had had to contend with such difficult issues as the outbreak of the Korean War—had told the press, "I shall take all the troubles of the past, all the disappointments, all the headaches, and I shall pack them in a bag and throw them in the East River."[2]

Lie's successors would be likely to share this cheerful assessment. If anything, the UNSG's position became even more difficult over succeeding decades as the membership of the UN enlarged and diversified. Yet some of them have left a significant legacy. Dag Hammarskjöld, for example, championed the creation of UN peacekeeping forces, those with the blue helmets who have patrolled the world's conflict regions over the past half a century. He also helped push economic development to the forefront of the UN's agenda. To be sure, Hammarskjöld's tenure coincided with the rapid explosion of UN membership as the decolonization process unfolded in the late 1950s and early 1960s. Personally committed to making the UN a significant player in world affairs, Hammarskjöld did not let the UN become completely hostage to Cold War antagonisms that threatened to expand to the newly independent parts of the globe. Hammarskjöld died in a plane crash in 1961— and thus achieved a martyrdom of sorts—in the midst of the Congo crisis, one of the many conflicts that arose from this process.

Most subsequent Secretaries-General have not enjoyed the same public exposure, in part because the ongoing Cold War and the

UN Secretaries-General

1946–52	Trygve Lie, Norway
1953–61	Dag Hammarskjöld, Sweden
1961–71	U Thant, Myanmar (Burma)
1972–81	Kurt Waldheim, Austria
1982–91	Javier Pérez de Cuéllar, Peru
1992–96	Boutros Boutros-Ghali, Egypt
1997–2006	Kofi Annan, Ghana
2007–	Ban Ki-moon, Republic of Korea (South Korea)

explosion of membership made administering the UN increasingly difficult. The choice of the UNSG also remained a highly sensitive issue; since each of the P-5 had a veto on the matter, the selection resulted in a series of compromises that while spreading the right to hold the post beyond Northern Europe, also produced relatively ineffective UNSG's: the Burmese U. Thant, the Austrian Kurt Waldheim, the Peruvian Pérez de Cuéllar, and the Egyptian Boutros Boutros-Ghali. To be fair, all of these men (and so far all UNSGs have been men) did attempt to maintain the impartiality and high profile of their office as best they could. But Cold War prerogatives and, in the case of Boutros-Ghali, preponderant American influence in the 1990s, doomed any effort to lift the UN's independent profile.

In the end, the next UNSG to stand out as having left a significant mark on the organization is the Ghanaian Kofi Annan. During his tenure the UN adopted the so-called Millennium Goals, a broad set of guidelines aimed at cutting global poverty in half by 2015. Annan also started and spearheaded a process of incremental reform of the administrative management structure of the UN, aimed at making the UN a more effective organization. But perhaps most importantly, the soft-spoken and always charming Annan managed to keep the UN's image relatively positive at a time when its relevance—and the integrity of its staff—was increasingly questioned. Like Hammarskjöld, Annan, the first UNSG who was a career UN official, was awarded the Nobel Peace Prize. Still, the last few years of Annan's time in office were hampered by numerous challenges, such as the conflict over the American-led invasion of Iraq, the inability of the UN to forge a quick end to the fighting that erupted on the Israeli-Lebanese border in 2006, and charges of widespread corruption within the UN system (which involved, among others, Annan's own son). To Annan, vacating the UNSG's office in New York upon the arrival of Ban Ki-moon in December 2006 must have been a relief of sorts.

Indeed, the Secretariat and the UNSG's office are hampered by numerous problems, including bureaucratic intransigence, red tape, budgetary shortfalls, and mismanagement. Most significantly, the last six decades have shown the difficulties in maintaining an international staff within a system that makes the Secretariat, like so much of the UN, dependent on the whims of the P-5. Moreover, any effort at streamlining the UN faces a virtually insurmountable challenge in the plethora of organizations that make up the often dysfunctional UN family.

A further difficulty for UN reform efforts stems from its uniqueness: its universal membership. Beneath the often high-minded rhetoric at the General Assembly and the Security Council lay layer upon layer of competing national ambitions and agendas. The multinational staff overseen by the Secretary-General is supposed to rise above such pettiness, but in reality this is virtually impossible. At a practical level, the members of the Secretariat bring with them their own cultural and national management styles, work ethics, and cultural preferences that can, in turn, create severe interpersonal conflict and hurt the effectiveness of the given UN bureau or field office. The observance of national and religious holidays—to give a simple example—may at times coincide with important meetings and conferences. Ironically, finding ways of avoiding intercultural tension is not just one of the mandates stipulated in the UN's Charter; it is part of the daily life within the organization itself.

ECOSOC and the three sisters

Under the UN's mandate, the Economic and Social Council (ECOSOC) "coordinates the economic and social work of the United Nations and the UN family of organizations" and therefore "plays a key role in fostering international cooperation for development." That sounds fine and logical. The SC was charged with weighty issues of military security, leaving ECOSOC to deal with the related questions of economic security. These were not to be taken lightly, for many of the negotiators involved in the drafting of the UN Charter saw the economic depression of the 1930s as the root cause of World War II.

In truth ECOSOC is a relatively powerless part of the UN structure. With fifty-four members representing more than a quarter of the total UN roster of nations, each elected by the General Assembly for three-year terms (on the basis of "equitable geographical representation"), ECOSOC oversees a number of functional (such as Human Rights, Sustainable Development) and regional commissions. The Commission on Human Rights, for example, monitors the observance of human rights throughout the world (and the work of the new Human Rights Council and, before 2006, the Office of the High Commissioner for Human Rights). Other bodies focus on social development, the status of women, crime prevention, narcotic drugs, and environmental protection. Five regional commissions promote economic development and cooperation in their respective areas. But ECOSOC's mission remains as amorphous as its structure.

In fact, the true global economic power within the UN family lies with the so-called three sisters: the World Bank, the International

Presidents of World Bank*	Managing Directors of IMF
Eugene Meyer, 1946	Camille Gutt (Belgium), 1946–51
John J. McCloy, 1947–49	Ivar Rooth (Sweden), 1951–56
Eugene R. Black, 1949–63	Per Jacobsson (Sweden), 1956–63
George D. Woods, 1963–68	Pierre-Paul Schweitzer (France), 1963–73
Robert McNamara, 1968–81	Johannes Witteveen (Netherlands), 1973–78
Alden W. Clausen, 1981–86	Jacques de Larosiere (France), 1978–87
Barber Conable, 1986–91	Michel Camdessus (France), 1987–2000
Lewis T. Preston, 1991–95	Horst Köhler (Germany), 2000–04
James Wolfensohn, 1995–2005	Rodrigo Rato y Figaredo (Spain), 2004–
Paul Wolfowitz, 2005–07	
Robert Zoellick, 2007–	

*all U.S. citizens

Monetary Fund (IMF), and the World Trade Organization (WTO). Each has its own specific remit. Based in Washington, the World Bank, originally known as the International Bank for Reconstruction and Development, is a multilateral institution that lends money to governments and government agencies for development projects. The IMF, also located in Washington, lends money to governments to help stabilize currencies and maintain order in international financial markets. The WTO, headquartered in Geneva, was founded in 1995 to replace the General Agreement on Tariffs and Trade (GATT). Its general goal is to lower tariffs and other trade barriers.

Together the three sisters wield tremendous power and influence but also attract criticism as organizations that favor the established free-market system over any possible alternatives. Indeed, the rules of governance within the organizations give certain countries a clear advantage in decision making. At the World Bank and the IMF voting power is weighted based on individual countries' contributions. This means that the United States has (in 2005) approximately 17 percent of the vote while the seven major industrialized countries (G-7: Britain, Canada, France, Germany, Italy, Japan, and the United States) together hold about 45 percent. No one-country, one-vote principle here! In fact, the biggest "shareholder," the United States, has always held effective veto power over the World Bank and IMF's decisions. The Western dominance over these institutions has been strengthened further by the long-standing tradition of choosing an American as the president of the World Bank, and a European as the managing director of the IMF.

The problem that stems from this structure is evident. The countries that have most at stake—the countries in the developing world that are often in need of World Bank loans or IMF credits—have relatively little power within these institutions. But the programs and policies that are decided upon in Washington often have a tremendous impact throughout the developing world. It is no wonder that the critics of the IMF and the World Bank argue that they represent a new form of Western control over Africa, parts of Asia, the Middle East, and Latin America. (In the last region, Venezuelan president Hugo Chavez has championed the creation of Banco del Sur [Bank of the South], as a way of ridding South America from dependency on World Bank loans and U.S. dominance.)

The WTO (and its predecessor GATT) is seemingly more democratic than its Washington-based sisters. Voting is not weighted. Decisions are made—or often not made—by consensus (majority voting is possible but has never been used). However, given the broad array of members (more than 75 percent of the total of 153 countries are from the developing world) with different interests and goals, the need to find a consensus inevitably leads to heavy behind-the-scenes bargaining. In such discussions, though, American and European representatives (or the so-called G-7 countries) clearly start from a strong position vis-à-vis, say, countries in Africa. Leverage— economic or political—matters, albeit in a different way as in the context of the IMF or the World Bank.

The basic point is that the WTO yields little power of its own; it is the member states that decide through a lengthy bargaining process over changes in multilateral trading rules. And since some member states ultimately are more equal than others, the WTO, much like its sisters, is often charged with an effort to perpetuate an international economic system dominated by the North.

Programs, funds, specialized agencies

As noted earlier, ECOSOC is responsible for coordinating the social work of the UN. This translates to a loose role as the overseer of the work carried out by a large number of specialized agencies, programs, and funds. Some of these—especially the many humanitarian organizations—are well known and held in high regard. Most everyone would have heard, for example, about the UN International Children's Fund (UNICEF) or the World Health Organization (WHO).

A full listing of all the various organizations—many of which will be discussed in other chapters—would make this book much more than a "very short introduction." (See chart 2.1.) But it is worth asking: what, aside from the issues they address, differentiates a "Specialized Agency" (like the WHO) from the group "Programs and Funds" (like UNICEF)?

Part of the answer is simple: money. While Programs and Funds are financed mainly through voluntary contributions from member countries (making their finances chronically uncertain), the Specialized Agencies are funded through a mixture of assessments (i.e., contributions from the overall UN budget) and voluntary contributions. The latter have a baseline budget, the former do not. Some countries are indeed more equal than others at the UN Security Council and the World Bank; but Specialized Agencies are more equal than Programs and Funds.

The practical consequences of such systemic division are controversial. One is justified in asking, for example, why UNICEF should be required to spend more of its time in fundraising to assist disadvantaged children than the UN Educational, Scientific, and Cultural Organization (UNESCO) is required in planning its activities to enhance intercultural understanding? Why does the World Tourism Organization (WTO, not to be confused with the other WTO) enjoy greater stability as a specialized agency than does the office of the UN High Commissioner for Refugees (UNHCR)? The latter does, after all, address the needs of roughly 20 million refugees, internally displaced people, and asylum seekers!

These are questions we will revisit in the final chapter of this book. They do, however, point to another basic question related to the UN structure: How much does it all cost?

Footing the bill: who pays and how much?

The popular notion is that the roughly $20 billion that the various UN operations cost in 2006 make it a prohibitively expensive enterprise. Yet, before coming to this conclusion, one might consider a few salient facts. First, the UN's total budget represents but a fraction of most countries' national budgets; indeed, the UN total expenditures are roughly the same as those of the country with the highest per capita income in the world, Luxembourg (a population of less than 500,000).

UN funding is unduly complex—almost like another Picasso abstraction. In very general terms, however, the UN budget is based on two categories of contributions: assessed (ca. 45 percent in 2006) and voluntary (55 percent). The assessed contributions can, in turn, be divided into three categories according to the end use of the funds:

1. Assessed contributions to the Regular Operating Budget (totaling about $1.8 billion in 2006)
2. Assessed contributions to UN Specialized Agencies (ca. $2 billion)
3. Assessed contributions to UN Peacekeeping Operations (ca. $5 billion)

The basic rule in "assessing" how much each member country should contribute to the UN is simple: the wealthier the country is, the more it must pay. There is, though, a ceiling for wealthy countries and a minimum for the poorer ones. The maximum contribution for any single country is 22 percent of the entire operating budget. This is what the United States (which represents more than 30 percent of the world economy) contributes. The minimum contribution is 0.001 percent, paid (if not defaulted) by such countries as Laos, Malawi, and Timor-Leste. A similar scale of assessment is used to raise the $2 billion that fund the operations of the various specialized agencies. The largest recipients in this category are the World Health Organization (WHO) with $458 million, Food and Agricultural Organization (FAO) with $377 million, UNESCO with $306 million, International Atomic Energy Agency (IAEA) with $276 million, and ILO with $265 million.

At 25–27 percent of the total, the United States is also the largest single contributor to peacekeeping costs. The higher assessment for peacekeeping operations is explained by an important modification: for peace operations the permanent members of the Security Council pay proportionately more than for the regular budget. Conversely, the floor for the least developed countries is even lower than for the regular budget (0.0001 percent).

UN Operating Budget

The major contributors to the UN operating budget of about $4.2 billion are assessed based on the proportion of their national economy vis-à-vis the size of the global economy. In 2000 the UN lowered the ceiling of these contributions from 25% to 22% of the total budget. In 2005–06 this meant that the top ten contributors to the UN operating budget were ranked as follows (China and Mexico were new entries into the "top ten").

1.	United States	22.00%
2.	Japan	19.47%
3.	Germany	8.66%
4.	UK	6.13%
5.	France	6.03%
6.	Italy	4.89%
7.	Canada	2.81%
8.	Spain	2.52%
9.	China	2.05%
10.	Mexico	1.80%

Some member nations are in arrears on their payments, most notably the United States. The European Union countries contribute roughly 35% of the total operating budget. Special UN programs—such as UNICEF and UNDP—are not included in the regular budget and are financed by voluntary contributions from member governments.

The amount of assessed contributions to the regular budget is set every three years by the General Assembly. In addition to the United States, the other major contributors include Japan, Germany, United Kingdom, France, Italy, Canada, Spain, and China. Indeed, these nine countries combined pay for roughly 75 percent of the entire core budget of the United Nations.

Voluntary contributions were estimated at roughly $10 billion in 2006. Although most of this goes for the various Programs and

Funds, some of the contributions benefit the work of the various Specialized Agencies (the difference between the funding of UN Programs and Funds as opposed to Specialized Agencies has already been touched upon previously). Exceptions among the Specialized Agencies are the IMF and the World Bank, which are funded and governed outside of the UN system. This, naturally, gives them an added degree of independence (or dependence from the major funding countries). It also makes them far wealthier. The World Bank, for example, had an operating budget of more than $2 billion in 2007 and approved in 2005 more than $22 billion in loans and credits to various development projects.

All of this translates into a few uncomfortable facts. First, the UN depends on the contributions of its wealthiest member states, particularly the United States. Second, this dependency gives the "big payers"—especially because they are (with the exception of Russia) also permanent members of the Security Council—an effective stranglehold on the overall ability of the UN to function at all. Or if it is to function, the wealthy contributors can exercise (perhaps) undue influence on the direction of the UN's policies. Third, the developing countries that are most in need of the UN's assistance are thus indirectly linked via a "dependency chain" to the continued goodwill of the most developed ones.

A penniless hybrid? A dysfunctional family?

The complexity of the UN is its strength and its weakness. While the UN has a body (at least one) or a related organization devoted to almost any imaginable issue, it can be extremely cumbersome when it comes to dealing with specific issues or solving complex problems. There are bureaucratic conundrums. As in any large organization, turf battles within and among different agencies can reach epic proportions. There is duplication of services and, as many critics argue, too much political correctness: an uncalled-for emphasis for satisfying national quotas over actual skills when making appointment decisions within the various UN organizations.

An additional symptom of the UN's complexity is the uncertainty of funding that hampers its operational abilities. At the very basic level, the UN relies on its wealthiest member states to fund its operations. These contributions are in no case massive (in the case of the United States it represents less than 0.25 percent of the federal budget) and they often come in late, if at all. At the end of 2006 member states owed the UN $2.3 billion (the United States counted for 43 percent of this amount). The UN operates, it seems, permanently in the red.

But what has this hybrid, penniless structure achieved since 1945? Where has it been successful? Where has it failed? How can it be improved? Is there any sense of discussing it as anything else than a Picasso abstraction?

Chapter 3

Facing wars, confronting threats: the UN Security Council in action

If the purpose of the UN was to save mankind from the destruction that had overshadowed the history of the first half of the twentieth century, measuring its success depends on one's perspective. On the one hand, it could be argued that since no World War III has erupted, the founders had created a successful organization. On the other hand, not a day has gone by since 1945 without a deathly military conflict somewhere on the globe. Many such conflicts have transpired and continued with the full knowledge of the United Nations Security Council (UNSC). In short, the UN may have played a role in saving mankind from the devastation of global war, but it has not come close to eliminating the scourge of war from our planet.

Nor is it clear whether the absence of global military confrontation has had much to do with the UN and its executive body, the Security Council. It can be argued that the existence and proliferation of nuclear weapons acted as a deterrent against a direct military confrontation between the United States and the Soviet Union. The potential consequences of such a war—a rapid annihilation of one's own country—removed the incentive to go to war far more effectively than any deliberations at the UN. But the United States and the USSR were more than happy to intervene in military conflicts around the globe that did not seem likely to escalate into a direct superpower confrontation. After the Cold

War new antagonisms emerged, most evidently within the context of the United States' call for regime change in Iraq in 2002–03.

This does not mean that the Security Council was or is irrelevant. It simply underlines the fact that at its very founding, this central organ of the UN could be effective only when the so-called P-5 were in agreement. In fact, the UNSC has on numerous occasions exercised an important role as a global troubleshooter. Taking into account the dependence of the UNSC on the unanimity of its five permanent members—and hence on the national interests of China, France, Great Britain, Russia (formerly the Soviet Union), and the United States—it has actually been remarkably successful and active. Ideally, the Security Council's role should not be purely reactive. It should also be able to address potential threats and prevent them from materializing. The relationship between UNSC and the International Atomic Energy Agency (IAEA), sometimes referred to as the UN's "nuclear watchdog," is a good example of the potential that the UN has for making a positive impact on international security in the twenty-first century. There is probably no other issue besides the possibility of a nuclear holocaust to bring peoples and countries together. Yet the attempt to safeguard against the proliferation of such weapons has been a half-hearted success at best. Once again, national interests have clashed with global security concerns to produce a series of imperfect compromises and temporary solutions.

Political constraints: the veto conundrum

In theory, the Security Council has few limits to its power. Its remit is broad; its resolutions are binding on all members of the UN. In short, if the UNSC decided something—to impose sanctions against a country or to enforce a ceasefire in a conflict area—the order would have to be implemented. One could not, in other words, ignore the collective will of the P-5 that effectively determines the decisions of the UNSC. But finding such collective will has often been an elusive quest. The question of national

Box 3.1 Veto power ("Great Power unanimity")

Each UN Security Council member has one vote. Decisions on procedural matters (for example, whether an issue is to be discussed by the UNSC at all) require the support of at least nine of the fifteen members. Decisions on substantive matters (for example, a decision calling for direct measures to settle an international dispute, or to employ sanctions) also require nine votes, but these must include the votes of all five permanent members. This is the rule of "Great Power unanimity," often referred to as the "veto" power.

In theory the nonpermanent members of the UNSC also hold a collective veto power: if at least seven of them vote collectively against a resolution (whether procedural or substantive) they can block a resolution even if all the permanent members vote for it. This so-called sixth veto has existed only since 1965, when the number of nonpermanent members was increased from six to ten. Although all P-5 members have used their veto power repeatedly, the sixth veto has yet to be employed.

sovereignty is at the top of the list, and it is something that those who are "more equal" than others—that is, the P-5—hold particularly dear. And since they have the right to veto decisions, they are likely to do so should a proposed resolution be against their national interest.

The P-5's right of veto has complicated the UNSC's work more than any other issue. Indeed, the fact that five nations—out of a total of 192—have a privileged position seems absurd. If the People's Republic of China (and, more absurdly, between 1949 and 1971 the small island of Taiwan, known as the Republic of China), France, Great Britain, Russia, and the United States can agree on a course, then the UN can act. If they do not—or if only *one* of them decides that a certain resolution is objectionable—then the UNSC is effectively paralyzed.

Thus, the use of the veto can actually prevent the UN from enforcing measures to end a war. This was the case, for example, in December 1971, when the Soviet Union vetoed a UN resolution calling for a ceasefire in a war between India and Pakistan. By doing so the Soviets were helping India to continue its military advances against Pakistan, a firm American ally in the Cold War. Truth be told, Pakistan had won few friends because of its repression of an independence movement in what was soon to become the independent nation of Bangladesh (but was until 1971 formally known as East Pakistan). Yet the Pakistani government was perfectly within its rights when it complained that the international community was failing to enforce a peaceful resolution and, in effect, left the outmaneuvered Pakistanis no alternative but to surrender (which they did on December 16,

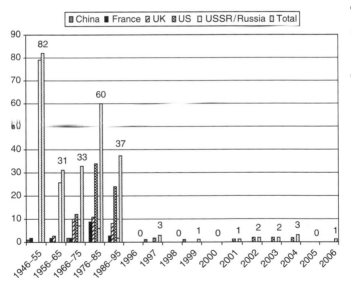

Chart 3.1 Use of the Veto.

During the Cold War the USSR was the most frequent user of the veto. After first using it in 1970, however, the United States has taken over this role. Yet, as the chart shows, the P-5 have almost ceased exercising this privilege since the end of the Cold War.

1971). Witnessing his country's hardships from New York, Zulfikar Ali Bhutto, the foreign minister of Pakistan, erupted in front of a UN Security Council meeting: "Let's build a monument for the veto. Let's build a monument for impotence and incapacity."[1]

To be sure, the General Assembly has often issued resolutions despite a P-5 veto. But such resolutions simply do not carry the authority necessary to outweigh a stubborn permanent UNSC member. Nor does the fact that the nonpermanent members of the UNSC hold a theoretical "sixth veto" since the expansion of Security Council membership in the 1960s make the body either more effective or less driven by great power prerogatives.

The UNSC, for better or worse, was and remains an arena of power and realpolitik. And despite attempts to reform it, the body remains, after six decades, more or less the way it was at the founding: empowered in theory but incapacitated in practice.

Operational constraints: the Military Staff Committee

In order to prevent wars and stop the ones that did erupt, the UN needed a military capacity. How else could the organization throw its weight around but by dispatching troops to a troubled region? How else could the UN force warring parties—unwilling to yield to diplomatic or economic pressure—to cease fighting but by displaying superior military prowess?

The UN Charter addressed these questions. It set up the Military Staff Committee (MSC) as a subsidiary body of the Security Council and charged it with the planning of UN military operations. The MSC was further mandated to assist the Security Council in arms regulation (including, implicitly, the regulation of nuclear arms). Moreover, the MSC was to provide the command staff for a set of air force contingents provided by the P-5. The contingents themselves were to be scattered on UN bases around the globe so that the Security Council could call upon them as needed.

The problem with this plan soon became evident. None of the P-5 saw an independent military force serving their interests. The mistrust and tensions of the early Cold War—including the creation of such military alliances as NATO and the Warsaw Pact—meant that none of the P-5 provided the required forces. Already in July 1948—following two years of negotiations—the MSC reported to the Security Council that it was unable to fulfill its mandate.

Consequently, although it was the only subsidiary body of the Security Council mentioned in the charter, the MSC became "dormant" (or irrelevant, in non-UN language). To be sure, there was a brief revival of interest in the MSC in 1990 when it played a role in coordinating naval operations during the Gulf War. In the end, however, the UN has shifted toward subcontracting force out to regional bodies such as NATO (for example in Kosovo) or the African Union (in Darfur) rather than creating a structured and effective military capacity of its own.

After sixty years the MSC still exists as an advisory body that plays a role in the planning and conduct of UN peacekeeping operations. It consists of army, naval, and air force representatives of the P-5. This group meets every two weeks at the UN headquarters in New York. Other UN members are included in meetings regarding peacekeeping operations in which their country's forces are deployed. But the practical significance of the MSC remains, as it always has been, extremely limited.

Political constraints: Security Council and the Cold War

The record of the UNSC is checkered. To be sure, it deliberated on virtually all international conflicts during the Cold War, such as the Arab-Israeli wars, Korea, Suez, Congo, and Berlin. In all those cases, however, it was contingency—the specific interests of the P-5 (and especially the United States and the Soviet Union)—rather than the principles of the UN Charter that ultimately decided the outcome.

While the veto power of the P-5 extends to a number of areas—including the choice of the UN Secretary-General or the admission of new members to the UN—what truly counts is the way in which the P-5's privileged position has affected the UN's ability in matters related to war and peace. Of course, the line even here has often been blurred and the actual measures taken—and resolutions passed or not passed—depended ultimately how and if the interests of the P-5 were influenced by the conflict in question.

For example, the first Soviet use of the veto, in February 1946, was over a resolution regarding the withdrawal of French forces from Syria and Lebanon. The Soviet UN ambassador argued that the regimes slated to take over these countries were essentially French puppet governments. Later in the same year, the UNSC refused to discuss a Siamese complaint about French military activities on its border with Indochina and could not come to an agreement over an investigation regarding the communist-royalist civil war in Greece.

The major division within the Security Council's P-5 was, though, straightforward and reflected the emergence of the Cold War. On most issues where the veto was used, the Soviet Union stood on one side, the other four members on the other. This, effectively, guaranteed a deadlock on most issues, including such hot concerns as the division of Berlin. In June 1948, the USSR—which occupied East Germany, including all areas surrounding Berlin, after the war—cut off all land connections and supply routes to West Berlin. The American, British, and French forces occupying that part of the German capital (as well as the Germans who lived there) were, essentially, hostages. To overcome the blockade, the United States commenced a massive airlift of food and other supplies. It would last almost a year.

6. A 1953 cartoon illustrates the struggle between Mao Zedong, chairman of the Communist Party in Communist China, and Chiang Kai-Shek, president of Nationalist China, for the "China seat" in the UN.

The Berlin blockade of 1948–49 dramatically illustrated the limits of the UNSC's influence. While the Western powers debated and drafted resolutions to end the blockade, the Soviets ignored any possibility of compromise. Not until early 1949 did the Soviets accept that Western powers could not be smoked out of Berlin. After several months of negotiations between the American and Soviet ambassadors to the UN, an end to the blockade was finally announced in May 1949. But the crisis and its solution had illustrated that the UNSC was not likely to be an operational body. It could not prevent conflicts but could, however, provide a context for negotiating an end to a confrontation.

Within months after the end of the Berlin blockade, the UNSC faced a new conundrum: what to do with the Chinese membership after the communists triumphed in the Civil War and proclaimed the People's Republic of China (PRC) on October 1, 1949. To the Soviets, the obvious course was to replace the "old" China with the "new" one. But others—least of all the Chinese representative in the UNSC—disagreed, refusing even to recognize the legitimacy of the PRC. Instead, the Americans and others upheld the Republic of China (which had been reduced to the island of Taiwan) as the legitimate member of the P-5. By the summer of 1950, in a vain effort to sway the other P-5 members, the Soviets were boycotting the UNSC meetings. In 1971 the PRC finally gained its seat. At the same time Taiwan was summarily ejected from the world body.

The Korean conflict

On June 24, 1950, North Korean troops crossed into South Korea. The UNSC was able to pass an American-drafted resolution condemning the attack because Jakob Mali, the Soviet ambassador, was not in New York to veto it. Another resolution authorized the use of force to push the North Koreans back. The preeminently American troops that carried out the resolution eventually overstepped the boundaries of the UNSC resolution by moving deep into North Korea (and very close to the Chinese border) in the fall of 1950. The Chinese intervened, and the conflict dragged on for several years.

Far from strengthening the UN's effectiveness, the Korean conflict may actually have diminished it. The arrival of mostly American troops under American command (led by General Douglas MacArthur) spoke of the futility of expecting rapid military action from the world body unless a member state was ready to step in and pick up the responsibility. The United States—with the help of a number of other countries—did so from 1950 to 1953. But it was clear that for the Americans the Korean conflict was primarily an American war fought to contain the expansion of communism rather than a call for duty under the UN charter.

The Korean conflict also produced an important resolution that, at least in theory, provided a challenge to the executive authority of the Security Council. In November 1950 the General Assembly passed Resolution 377, also known as the "United for Peace" Resolution. It stated that in case the UNSC could not maintain international peace, an issue could be taken up by the General Assembly. Although seemingly revolutionary, the resolution was promoted by the United States as a way of circumventing possible Soviet vetoes—the USSR having returned to the UN in the meantime—regarding Korea. It became clear over the years that followed, however, that notwithstanding Resolution 377, the General Assembly remained subservient to the Security Council.

United Nations General Assembly Resolution 377, November 3, 1950

"[I]f the Security Council, because of lack of unanimity of the permanent members, fails to exercise its primary responsibility for the maintenance of international peace and security in any case where there appears to be a threat to the peace, breach of the peace, or act of aggression, the General Assembly shall consider the matter immediately with a view to making appropriate recommendations to Members for collective measures, including in the case of a breach of the peace or act of aggression the use of armed force when necessary, to maintain or restore international peace and security."

Among the many other lessons of the Korean conflict one stands out. The P-5 learned that absence from the UNSC could be costly to their national interest. The Soviets would not miss future meetings (naturally, the other four UNSC members learned the same lesson). This had two consequences. It highlighted the importance of the UNSC as a means of blocking action that might jeopardize the interests of the P-5. No wonder that the next large-scale military action blessed by the UNSC would not take place until the end of the Cold War. In the more immediate term, though, the role of the UNSC as the place where all cold-war issues would be deliberated upon was secure.

Suez and the "P-2"

Korea was the sole case during the Cold War when the UNSC actually authorized a large-scale military intervention. There were plenty of other wars and conflicts that were consistently debated and voted upon. But after the Korean War such conflicts—and what the UN could do about them—were increasingly linked to the interplay between the gradual globalization of the Cold War and the simultaneous decolonization of European empires. In some cases, they produced odd bedfellows.

One example was the Suez crisis of 1956. In October of that year the British, French, and Israelis cooperated in an offensive against Egypt with the aim of removing Gamel Abdel Nasser from power. Among Nasser's sins was his decision to nationalize the Suez Canal, which had led to numerous discussions in the Security Council as well as a series of mediation efforts by Secretary-General Dag Hammarskjöld. Nothing worked. Finally, on October 29, 1956, Israeli forces invaded the Sinai peninsula. By previous agreement, the British and French called for a ceasefire and the withdrawal of Egyptian and Israeli forces ten miles from the Suez Canal. When Israel, as had been agreed, accepted and Egypt, as expected, rejected the ultimatum, British and French planes bombed Cairo and the Suez Canal region. A few days later, without consulting the UNSC, London and Paris sent troops, ostensibly to keep the peace.

Given the lukewarm support of the Soviet leadership to Nasser's Egypt, the British and French hardly expected strong American criticism. It came as a rude shock to London and Paris that the Eisenhower administration called for an immediate Security Council condemnation of the Israeli, British, and French action. The Council voted 7–2, the British and French being forced to use their vetoes for the first time. But while they formally blocked the resolution, the British and French agreed within weeks to remove all their troops in favor of a UN peacekeeping force (the UN Emergency Force, or UNEF).

Ultimately, Suez showed two salient facts. The resolution of the crisis was an indication of the fact that among the P-5 some were indeed more equal than others, basically, the P-2: the United States and the Soviet Union. But Suez also showed that the General Assembly, which strongly criticized the attacks on Egypt, actually carried more than symbolic weight. In the end, though, this may have made it even more difficult for the Security Council to act decisively in the Cold War era.

Deadlocked and paralyzed

The Soviet Union and the United States clearly acted during Suez with an eye on the world's public opinion. Both superpowers were trying to win allies among the newly independent (or about to be independent) states in Africa, Asia, and the Middle East. Yet, as the explosion of nonaligned countries would show, countries like Egypt were keener on striking their own course than aligning themselves with the two most powerful states on the globe.

This did not mean that Cold War contests disappeared from the agenda of the Security Council. During the 1962 Cuban missile crisis, for example, the U.S. ambassador to the UN, Adlai

Stevenson, challenged his Soviet counterpart vehemently during one of the most public confrontations between the superpowers' representatives. In front of the television cameras, Stevenson demanded that Valentin Zorin, the Soviet representative, admit to the presence of Soviet missiles in Cuba. "I am prepared to wait for my answer until hell freezes over," said Stevenson. When Zorin refused to answer, the American showed photographs that clearly established the presence of the missiles. Despite Stevenson's impressive performance, the UNSC played virtually no direct role in the final solution to the crisis. That task was left for back-channel Soviet-American diplomacy.

By this point the UNSC had acquired much the same role as the General Assembly in the Cold War context: it had become a forum for public relations. Resolutions were debated but—if they made it to the Security Council's agenda—they were usually vetoed by one or more of the P-5. French military action in Indochina and Algeria in the 1950s and early 1960s passed without UNSC intervention. During the 1960s and 1970s, the United States military involvement in Vietnam and neighboring countries drew worldwide condemnation. But there was no UNSC resolution calling for an American withdrawal. A decade or so later the Soviet Union sent its troops to Afghanistan, but despite global uproar no UN resolution was forthcoming. Other deadly conflicts in, for example, Angola, the Horn of Africa, and Cambodia were in practice ignored by the Security Council because they involved the interests of one or more of the P-5. In sum, during the Cold War the UNSC was heavily influenced, to some extent even paralyzed, by the East-West confrontation.

An active UNSC: from Iraq to Iraq

All seemed to change as the end of the Cold War ushered in a new era of UNSC activism. In 1988 alone the Council authorized five new peacekeeping missions; in the early 1990s such missions proliferated around the globe. With the absence of Cold War antagonisms the UN appeared to emerge as a major player in shaping a new world order, a term employed, yet again, by an American president.

The most significant event heralding George H. W. Bush's idea of a "new world order"—a term that had surfaced for the first time during Woodrow Wilson's efforts to revamp the international system by creating the League of Nations at the end of World War I—was the American-led but UN-sponsored military operation in the Persian Gulf. Following the Iraqi invasion and occupation of Kuwait in August 1990, the U.S. administration engineered a series of unanimous UNSC resolutions that ultimately authorized the dispatch of a large multinational military force to push the Iraqis out of Kuwait. With the participation of thirty countries, approximately 660,000 troops, and a massive air operation, the American-led coalition did just that by the end of February 1991.

Although Operation Desert Storm was successfully concluded and represented the largest UNSC-authorized military campaign, its consequences were contradictory for the UN. On the one hand, the operation's success undoubtedly encouraged the UNSC to approve other, much smaller-scale military missions in the early 1990s. But the fact that a number of these missions—in former Yugoslavia, in Somalia, in Rwanda—could not quell the violence or stop genocide, highlighted the UN's continued lack of a reliable military arm. Far from increasing the credibility of the UN, the Gulf War actually undermined it.

More important, the Gulf War symbolized the inequality that was evident even among the UN's P-5. The sudden emergence of virtual unanimity among the veto powers did not hide the fact that there was, at this point, but one superpower. The United States—in part because of its dramatic advantages in wealth and military resources, in part because of the demise of its only true counterweight, the Soviet Union—emerged in the 1990s as the one power that could make or break any UNSC initiative.

Most disturbingly, in 2003 the United States showed that, as before, it could easily take massive military action without UNSC blessing. The occasion was, again, Iraq. Despite more than a decade of UN sanctions, that country was reportedly continuing to develop weapons of mass destruction (WMD). Iraq, still ruled by Saddam Hussein, arguably also had links to various terrorist groups, including Al Qaeda, the organization that had perpetrated the September 11, 2001, attacks in New York and Washington, D.C. Although both accusations proved false and the threat of a French veto led the United States to stop pushing for a UNSC resolution, the second U.S.-led invasion toppled Sadddam Hussein's government in the spring of 2003.

The comparison regarding the role of the UN in the two Gulf wars was stark. In 2003, the UN was reduced to the role of a bystander, called in—if at all—to engage in some humanitarian tasks after the "serious" military mission was completed. Nor was this the only such occasion to occur in the new millennium: in October 2001 the United States had led a military operation that toppled the Taliban government in Afghanistan (accused of harboring the headquarters of the terrorists who had planned the attacks of September 11). The UN was brought in afterwards, as a sponsor of the planning for the future shape of Afghanistan.

In short, the sudden activism—and apparent unanimity—of the UNSC in the early 1990s had not translated to the creation of a collective body that was willing to engage in the world's trouble spots after multilateral consultation. If anything, the end of the Cold War had highlighted the disparity between one of the P-5 countries and the rest of the world. When the UN engaged in various peace operations, it did so only in places that lacked obvious significance to the P-5, particularly the United States. The majority of UN members did not approve of the military action called for by the United States, but they were incapable of preventing it. In this sense, the collapse of the Cold War international system had changed little.

Nuclear threats and the IAEA

A key dimension in the field of international security after 1945 was the emergence of nuclear weapons. Indeed, the very first UN General Assembly resolution, adopted in January 1946, called for the elimination of "weapons adaptable to mass destruction" and cooperation toward harnessing the peaceful use of atomic energy.

Broad principles, however, again clashed with naked national interest. The United States chose to safeguard its monopoly of atomic weapons, while the Soviet Union quickly moved to develop its own arsenal. By the fall of 1949 the USSR had successfully tested one. By 1964, after the People's Republic of China tested its weapon, all of the P-5 were members of the nuclear club (Great Britain and France had conducted their first tests in the interim period). In subsequent decades India and Pakistan both declared their nuclear capabilities, while other states—Israel, Iran, and North Korea—worked hard to acquire them. Many others—from South Africa to Sweden—flirted with the idea of developing their own nuclear weapons at some stage.

The justification, in all cases, has been deterrence rather than offense. The possession of nuclear weapons presumably makes a state invulnerable to attacks from other states, the consequences— a subsequent retaliation with nuclear weapons—being too grave to the attacker. And indeed, despite such tense moments as the 1962 Cuban missile crisis, nuclear weapons have not been used since the United States dropped two atomic bombs on Japan in 1945. At that point, of course, the bombs were used for offensive purposes and without the fear of retaliation in kind.

Although nuclear weapons have not been used as a tool of war for more than six decades, the proliferation of nuclear weapons is proof of the overall failure—especially by the P-5—to live up to the 1946 UN goal of abolishing nuclear weapons. There have been many efforts to control their spread by the International Atomic Energy Agency (IAEA), founded in 1957 and headquartered in Vienna. As well, a series of international treaties has been aimed at controlling the proliferation of nuclear weapons, at limiting the scale of the arsenals each country holds, and, ultimately, at bringing the threat of nuclear war under control.

The IAEA grew from an American proposal in December 1953 that eventually resulted in the unanimous approval of the agency's statute by the General Assembly in October 1956. An independent agency, the IAEA reports regularly to both the GA and the UNSC on its work, which focuses on three areas: nuclear verification and security, nuclear safety, and nuclear technology transfer. The recipient of the 2005 Nobel Peace Prize, the IAEA is among the most high-profile UN agencies and its Director General (in 2008 the Egyptian diplomat Mohammed ElBaradei) ranks as one of the most publicly visible UN functionaries.

Such name recognition and international influence have not always been the case. Throughout the Cold War the IAEA remained a relatively impotent organization, beholden to the whims of the great powers. Particularly in the field of nuclear arms control, what mattered were the views from Moscow and Washington (and to a lesser extent London, Paris, and Beijing). In the field of nuclear proliferation even the views from the great capitals could not prevent states bent on acquiring nuclear weapons capability from doing so.

The efforts at nuclear arms control were therefore essentially results of old-fashioned power politics rather than the moral pressure of the international community. In the aftermath of the 1962 Cuban missile crisis, for example, the United States and the USSR began seeking common ground. In 1972 their talks led to the SALT I agreement that put caps on the number of offensive nuclear weapons each side could have. In a separate agreement (the Anti-Ballistic Missile, or ABM, Treaty) signed at the same time the Americans and the Soviets essentially agreed to freeze the development of "defensive" nuclear weapons. Whether the agreements were primarily aimed at making the world a safer place, as its principal advocates piously argued is, however, open to question. It is clear, though, that the renewed atmosphere of Soviet-American tensions in the late 1970s resulted in a renewed nuclear arms race in the 1980s. And there was nothing the IAEA could do about it.

Meanwhile, the addition of China and France to the nuclear "club" in the 1960s led to growing support for international, legally binding commitments and comprehensive safeguards to stop the further spread of nuclear weapons. The first major result was the approval of the Treaty on the Non-Proliferation of Nuclear Weapons (NPT) in 1968. The NPT essentially froze the number of declared nuclear weapon states at five (the U.S., Russia, the UK, France, and China). Other states were required to forswear the nuclear weapons option and to conclude comprehensive safeguard agreements with the IAEA on their nuclear materials. In the 1970s the NPT was accepted by almost all of the key industrial countries and by the vast majority of developing countries.

In the early 1990s the dissolution of the Soviet Union lifted the nuclear shadow of the Cold War. In 1995 the NPT was made permanent, and in 1996 the UN General Assembly approved and opened for signature a Comprehensive Test Ban Treaty (CTB). But fears of global annihilation as a result of a superpower showdown were soon replaced by renewed concerns of proliferation. Discoveries or concerns over clandestine weapons programs in Iraq (where the suspicions proved unfounded in 2003) and North Korea, as well as concern over the future of the former Soviet Union's massive nuclear arsenal and possibilities of nuclear terrorism led to the strengthening of the IAEA's role; it became, in

The Nuclear Non-Proliferation Treaty

The Treaty on the Non-Proliferation of Nuclear Weapons, also called the Nuclear Non-Proliferation Treaty, was initially signed on July 1, 1968. Its aim was to limit the spread of nuclear weapons. By 2007, 189 states had signed the treaty, and only four states have completely opted out of the NPT. Of these, two (India and Pakistan) are confirmed nuclear powers (those who have openly tested nuclear weapons), and one is a presumed nuclear power (Israel). One further nuclear power, the Democratic Republic of Korea, ratified the treaty in 1985 but withdrew from it in 2005. In 1995 the treaty was extended indefinitely and without conditions.

NPT has had its successes. Several NPT signatories have given up nuclear weapons or nuclear weapons programs. For example, in the 1970s South Africa undertook a nuclear weapons program and may even have conducted a nuclear test in the Atlantic ocean. But it later renounced nuclear weapons and signed NPT in 1991. At about this time, several former Soviet republics destroyed or transferred to Russia the nuclear weapons inherited from the Soviet Union.

effect, a global nuclear watchdog, a UN verification agency working to ensure that nuclear energy is developed for peaceful purposes.

But the IAEA remains hostage to the national interests of select countries. It still lacks the ability to satisfy those who demand assurances against the further proliferation of nuclear weapons. The United States and its allies used the Iraqi nuclear weapons program as a reason for the invasion and occupation of that country in 2003 despite (accurate) statements by the IAEA that no such program existed. The agency could do little to prevent the North Koreans from developing their nuclear arsenal in the 1990s and 2000s. The IAEA has had little impact on the apparent Iranian quest to develop a nuclear weapon.

In the end, the IAEA cannot make states abandon their quest for nuclear weapons. It can inspect, deliver a verdict, and make a recommendation to the UN. But it is ultimately up to the UN Security Council to act upon such findings and recommendations. UNSC did so, for example, in March 2007 (and again in 2008) when it unanimously decided to strengthen economic sanctions against Iran to pressure that country into abandoning its nuclear program. Whether such a decision would have the desired—or the opposite—effect remains to be seen.

UNSC in a "unipolar" world

The UNSC has been and remains the victim of its own rules. The great conundrum was created by the necessity to make sure that the most powerful countries would join and remain members of the UN. Thus, the five major winners of World War II were granted special status as the P-5 of the Security Council and the only ones with individual veto power (the sixth veto is essentially a hypothetical one). This aspect makes the UN an undemocratic institution. But it has also guaranteed that, unlike the League of Nations in the 1930s, the UN has not seen major powers leave the organization in protest. They need not do so. They can paralyze the UN with a simple vote—and they have repeatedly done so.

As a result, the Security Council has an uncertain future. Stripped of the ability to rapidly deploy a military force of its own, it has relied excessively on great power contributions for large-scale military campaigns. No wonder that the ones undertaken so far—in Korea in the early 1950s and in the Persian Gulf in the early 1990s—took place in extraordinary political circumstances. Both were essentially American military operations, and as such, both also highlighted the fact that the inability to agree on a substantial role for the Military Staff Committee in the 1940s had paralyzed the UN.

The basic point that follows is that today's UN remains, essentially, dependent on the whims of the P-5 and the specific power constellations among them. At the moment this means that the P-5 is in danger of becoming the P-1, with the United States playing the role of a global hegemon, directing or blocking UN interventions as befits its national interests. It is hardly an ideal situation, made more acute with the challenge of nuclear proliferation. The fact that the country that will most likely join the nuclear club before 2010 is Iran may also increase tensions within the UNSC, some of whose members depend, for example, on Iran's oil as a key energy resource.

The UNSC, much like most of the world organization, is undoubtedly in need of reform. In fact, it is the lynchpin of reform activity. At this point, however, it is useful to remind ourselves of the fact that for all its faults and limitations, the UN Security Council has authorized numerous peacekeeping missions. While the so-called blue helmets' record is far from perfect, they have saved and altered thousands—probably millions—of lives around the globe over the past five decades. They deserve a closer look.

Chapter 4

Peacekeeping to peacebuilding

"Certainly the idea of an international police force effective against a big disturber of the peace seems today unrealizable to the point of absurdity." It was an unexpected line from Lester B. Pearson, delivered as part of his Nobel Peace Prize acceptance speech in December 1957. After all, peacekeeping is among the most visible roles that the UN plays on every continent (save North America). In the summer of 2008 there were twenty-two individual active missions, manned by approximately 90,000 soldiers from more than a hundred countries. Yet as Pearson, whose remarkable career included stints as Canada's foreign and prime minister, indicated, trust in the success of such operations has not always been excessively high.[1]

Indeed, as Pearson—who was at the time the Canadian representative at the UN and who can take much of the credit for the creation of the first large-scale peacekeeping force in 1956 (to protect the Suez Canal)—perceived half a century ago, the UN has not lived up to the high expectations of its founders. One statistic illustrates this fact: between 1948 and 1988 the UNSC had authorized only thirteen peacekeeping missions. In those same years a number of interstate and an increasing number of intrastate (or civil) wars took place around the globe. In 1982 alone, more than forty intrastate conflicts were under way.

7. When Lester Pearson, Canada's delegate to the UN, won the Nobel Peace Prize in 1957, the citation praised him, in part, for his consistently "realistic and positive attitude....Lester Pearson's vision is not that of a dreamer. He looks at life and the conditions of the world as they are, basing his conclusions on realities."

Cold War pressures, particularly the inability of the Security Council to agree on matters of war and peace in a charged East-West context, explain part of the imperfect record. But even after the Cold War, UN peacekeeping has been faced with numerous problems that have shattered the image of benevolence and neutrality that the world body is supposed to project. In the 1990s genocides (in Rwanda) and ethnic cleansing (in the former Yugoslavia) took place despite the presence of blue-helmeted forces in those areas.

If anything, UN peacekeepers face more formidable challenges today than they did when they first took to the field in the 1950s. This is mainly because peacekeeping is no longer just about standing between two hostile sides in order to pacify a war and allow diplomacy take its course. Today's peacekeeping activities–or "peace operations"—are far more complex in nature: keeping peace is not the same thing as making and building peace.

The UN Charter and peacekeeping

The UN Charter itself does not refer to "peacekeeping," but the concept developed (and became a central part of the UN's agenda) in later years. This was in part a result of the simple fact that the fifty-one founders of the UN rejected the idea that the organization could intervene in internal affairs of a country. Thus peacekeeping—which eventually meant placing military within the borders of a state for the specific purpose of blocking hostilities—could easily be regarded as a breach of national sovereignty. To guard against that possibility, "traditional"—or what is often referred to as "first generation"—peacekeeping was possible only with the consent of the hostile parties. Unfortunately this could also work in reverse: a "host" country could demand that the UN peacekeeping force exit its territory (for example, Egypt in 1967) or simply refuse them entry.

Nor did the UN have the means at its disposal for extensive peacekeeping missions. The idea of having permanent UN bases scattered around the world, originally envisioned in article 43 of the UN Charter, never got off the ground. Though this failure owed much to the emergence of Soviet-American rivalry in the immediate postwar years, it was also linked to the reality that the world of 1945 was governed with empires that assumed that they were entitled to play the role of a policing power within their "sphere." Countries such as Britain and France considered their imperial possessions as falling within the limits of their national sovereignty. In possession of the veto right in the UN Security

Council, they were in a position to block the establishment of anything resembling an international rapid-reaction force.

However, the swift dissolution of European empires in the aftermath of World War II created problems and conflicts that required a new kind of policing power. In 1947–48 the large-scale killings related to the partition of India and Pakistan, as well as the first Arab-Israeli War and the emergence of the Palestinian refugee issue, clearly indicated that the UN required a military arm if it was ever to subdue conflicts around the globe. These two crises resulted in the founding of the two longest-lasting UN peacekeeping missions: in May 1948 the United Nations Truce Supervision Organization (UNTSO) in the Middle East was established with headquarters in Jerusalem; in January 1949 the UN Military Observer Group in India and Pakistan (UNMOGIP) was deployed to monitor the ceasefire in the Kashmir region. Both were and remain small-scale observatory missions. Their extraordinary longevity is not a happy symbol for either region.

The Korean conflict of 1950 saw the deployment of the largest UN force in a conflict area. But the purpose of the American-dominated mission was to counter an attack that had already taken place, not to police a fragile peace. Less well known is the fact that UN peacekeepers remained on the South Korean side of the demilitarized zone until 1967, at which point U.S. and South Korean troops took over.

It was only in the mid-1950s that peacekeeping—"the first genuinely international police force," as Pearson put it—was born.

Suez and peacekeeping

The Egyptian nationalization of the Suez Canal in the summer of 1956 was followed by an Israeli invasion and Anglo-French intervention. With the UNSC paralyzed, the General Assembly passed a landmark resolution (GA Res. 998) on November 4, 1956

General Assembly Resolution 998

On November 4, 1956, the UN General Assembly adopted a Canadian proposal that requested, "as a matter of priority, the Secretary-General to submit to it within forty-eight hours a plan for the setting up, with the consent of the nations concerned, of an emergency international United Nations Force to secure and supervise the cessation of hostilities" along the Suez Canal. The vote was 57 to 0, with 19 abstentions. Egypt, France, Israel, the United Kingdom, the Soviet Union, and various eastern European states were among the abstainers.

authorizing the Swedish Secretary-General, Dag Hammarskjöld, to raise and deploy a UN Emergency Force (UNEF), responsible to Hammarskjöld and headed by a neutral officer. The proposal originated with Lester Pearson, who initially suggested that the force consist of mainly Canadian soldiers. But the Egyptians were suspicious of having a Commonwealth nation defend them against Great Britain and her allies. In the end, a wide variety of national forces were drawn upon to ensure national diversity. Pearson received the 1957 Nobel Peace Prize for his role and is today considered a father of modern peacekeeping.

The purpose of the 6,000-strong multinational peacekeeping force was straightforward: to erect a physical barrier between Israel and Egypt. It worked, if only for a decade. UNEF's presence depended on the consent of the regional (or host) nations. In 1967 Egyptian leader Gamal Abdel Nasser told UNEF to leave shortly before the so-called Six-Day War, during which Israel occupied the Sinai peninsula (as well as the Golan Heights and the West Bank).

The main significance of the Suez crisis from the perspective of the UN was as a prototype of modern peacekeeping. In numerous other conflicts after 1956, the blue helmets, worn mainly by soldiers from countries that were not among the P-5, would arrive and provide a shield against future hostilities. They would not be authorized to fire their guns except in self-defense.

As its name implies, UNEF was created simply to soothe an emergency situation. Its job was not to resolve the deeper sources of the conflict or enforce a permanent settlement. Moreover, the blue-helmeted soldiers who were stationed on the western part of the Sinai peninsula could be told to leave by their host country, Egypt, at any moment. In other words, peace could ultimately be kept only if those on either side of the conflict found it in their interest. A decade after the Suez conflict the Egyptians asked UNEF peacekeepers to leave on the eve of the Six-Day War. The repercussions of that 1967 conflict set the backdrop for the seemingly never-ending Israeli-Palestinian conflict.

Despite its limited long-term success, the prototype established at Suez was the general model used in most Cold War–era UN peacekeeping missions. The particular characteristics of this type of

"Generations" of peace operations

UN peacekeeping operations have greatly evolved in their purpose and complexity over the years. Observers thus like to divide them into three or four groups, usually referred to as "generations." Although the word is misleading in that implies a clear chronological progression rather than the parallel existence of several types of operations, the generations can roughly be defined as follows (this is not the only possible division; others talk of as many as six generations of peacekeeping):

First Generation peacekeeping (or traditional peacekeeping) refers to operations aimed at creating a physical barrier between two warring parties—both of them internationally recognized states—that have given their consent to peacekeepers' presence.

The classic example of this type of an operation is the role of the United Nations Emergency Force (UNEF) after the 1956 Suez crisis.

Second Generation peacekeeping (or peacebuilding) refers to the implementation of complex, multidimensional peace agreements, mostly in the aftermath of civil wars. Again the consent of the various parties is required, but they are usually not both (or all, if more than one) states. In addition to traditional military functions, peacekeepers play a role in various police and civilian functions. The goal is the long-term settlement of the underlying conflict. Examples of this type of operations include Namibia in 1989–90 and Cambodia in 1991–93.

Third Generation peacekeeping is often referred to as peace enforcement. These activities include low-level military operations, enforcing cease-fires, and rebuilding "failed states." The problem with the use of the term "generation" is particularly evident here: the Congo mission in the early 1960s was essentially the first example of peace enforcement, third generation peacekeeping actually predated the second generation ones. Two of the more recent examples of this type of operations are former Yugoslavia and Somalia in the 1990s.

Fourth Generation peacekeeping (rarely called such) refers to delegated peacebuilding when, for example, the UN subcontracts various peacebuilding and peacekeeping tasks to, say, regional organizations. Perhaps the best known example of this is NATO's role in Bosnia from the mid-1990s on.

"first generation" peacekeeping mission were their stringent neutrality and impartiality in the conflict in question, which allowed the UN and its member states to refrain from choosing sides. In an era characterized by the East-West rivalry, this was virtually the only way in which an international military mission could gain the support of states on opposite sides of the Cold War divide. However, the emphasis placed upon monitoring the situation, rather than influencing it, the need to have the consent of the conflicting parties, and the nonuse of force (except in self-defense) made the Suez prototype unfit for all types of conflict situations, particularly the many succession struggles that erupted in the aftermath of European decolonization in the 1950s and 1960s.

The birth of peace enforcement: the Congo

Although the Suez crisis set the pattern of modern UN peacekeeping in conflicts between nation-states, the Congo conundrum represented a new kind of challenge. The sudden independence of the former Belgian colony in early 1960 created not only the largest country in sub-Saharan Africa but one that was rife with internal power struggles, rich in resources, and ripe for external intervention. The richest province of the Congo, Katanga, declared itself independent after receiving support from Rhodesia and South Africa (both countries ruled by white minorities). When Belgian troops returned to the Congo, the country's prime minister, Patrice Lumumba, appealed to the UN for help. But the arrival of peacekeepers did not immediately solve the crisis as the UN Security Council debated the implications of intervention in the internal affairs of Congo, which had been a UN member state since September 1960.

The Congo became, in effect, the first case in which the UN was engaged in a "peace enforcement" mission. The 20,000-strong United Nations Operation in the Congo (Opération des Nations Unies au Congo, or ONUC) faced physical limitations and constant attacks from local groups. In the same year Patrice Lumumba was captured and killed by his internal opponents. The mayhem in Congo was almost total until 1964, when the unity of the country was—for the time being—restored and a central government headed by Mobutu Sese Seiko was firmly in power in Kinshasa. The last UN troops left the Congo in the summer of 1964. With 250

UN casualties, ONUC was the deadliest UN peacekeeping operation in the Cold War era. Among the casualties was the UN Secretary-General. Tragically, Dag Hammarskjöld's plane crashed in 1961 while he was shuttling around the region in an effort to mediate an end to the conflict.

The legacy of the UN's role in the Congo was mixed. Even though the ONUC played a role in ensuring the survival of the new nation as one unitary state, it had done little to solve the sources of future unrest and instability. Colonialism was gone, and the unity of what looked like a "failed state" had been preserved by the UN intervention. But the outcome was a corrupt dictatorship. Over three subsequent decades Mobutu proved a ruthless dictator, enriching his personal fortunes and favoring his support base while hiding behind the façade of a stable nation-state. Eventually in the 1990s, a lengthy civil war would ensue and Mobutu would be deposed. If peacekeeping à la Suez left the door open for interstate conflict, peace enforcement à la Congo provided no basis for future internal harmony.

Peacekeeping and Cold War constraints

Suez and the Congo were two examples of what might be termed the "prototypical" UN peacekeeping and peace enforcement missions. They were constrained by the ability of the Security Council's permanent members to veto any action if it seemed contrary to their national interest. Although Suez showed that even in cases where two of the P-5 were involved, the UN was indeed capable of some action; it was equally clear that without tremendous American and Soviet pressure nothing would have been done to curtail the interventions of Britain and France.

Suez remained an exception in this regard. During most of the Cold War era, until the late 1980s, UN peacekeeping and peace enforcement was not possible in a number of areas. During the bloody conflict in Algeria, for example, the UN was unable to intervene because of French ability to block any action. The

Vietnam wars—both its French (1946–54) and American (1960–75) phases—went by without the UN playing any significant role. When the Soviet Union invaded Afghanistan in 1979 or the Chinese attacked Vietnam in the same year, the UN could do nothing but offer to mediate. The lone mission in the Western Hemisphere—a region the United States continued to dominate—was established in the Dominican Republic in May 1965, following the unilateral military intervention by 20,000 U.S. marines. The Mission of the Representative of the Secretary-General in the Dominican Republic's (DOMREP) mandate lasted until October 1966, when its "infrastructure" (two military observers and a tiny civilian staff) was disbanded.

Still, the blue helmets expanded their operations even during the Cold War. From the 1960s to the 1980s, peacekeepers were sent to numerous conflict regions, particularly in the Middle East. Some of these operations have become part of the regional landscape. For example, the UN Peacekeeping Force in Cyprus (UNFICYP) has been present on the eastern Mediterranean island since 1964, and the UN Disengagement Observer Force (UNDOF) that was created to observe the border between Israel and Syria in 1974 still remains in place. Perhaps most astonishingly, the misnamed UN Interim Force in Lebanon (UNIFIL) was expanded in the summer of 2006 following the Israeli-Hezbollah conflict that threatened to destroy Lebanon's efforts to move toward some form of normality. UNIFIL was originally created in 1978. It has been a long "interim."

Overall, a total of eighteen UN peacekeeping missions were created during the Cold War. Unlike the few just cited, most were relatively short-lived. Several—the Dominican Republic one being an extreme example—were essentially observer missions. The good news was that fatalities were relatively few: between 1948 and 1990, 850 peacekeepers died. Moreover, UN forces diffused and "froze" a number of violent conflicts and, at a minimum, made negotiations between conflicting parties possible. By doing so, they saved lives and promoted the overall cause of peace; a much belated recognition of this role was the awarding of the Nobel Peace Prize to UN peacekeepers in 1988.

Nevertheless, as evidenced by the long-drawn-out conflicts in the Middle East and the ever-present UN observers in Kashmir, the impact that UN peacekeepers could have on the actual resolution

An Agenda for Peace, 1992

Former Secretary-General Boutros Boutros-Ghali's paper "An Agenda for Peace," which provided analysis and recommendations on ways to strengthen and improve the UN's capacity to maintain world peace, was commissioned by the UN Security Council on January 31, 1992, at its first-ever meeting at the level of heads of state.

"An Agenda for Peace" defined four consecutive phases of international action to prevent or control conflicts: Preventive diplomacy, Peacemaking, Peacekeeping, and Peacebuilding (action to identify and support indigenous structures that will help to strengthen and solidify peace in order to avoid a relapse into conflict).

The paper reflected an expanded outlook on the UN's role in the post–Cold War world, particularly in the area of UN peacekeeping. Instead of separating national armies involved in conflicts as had been the case during the Cold War, in the 1990s peacekeeping operations were deployed increasingly to situations of internal conflict, which involve nonstate or rebel forces (often calling themselves "national liberation movements"). The role(s) that peacekeepers have to perform in such conflicts are more complex than in traditional interstate conflicts. Further, "An Agenda for Peace" implied that, in order to intervene, the UN did not *necessarily* require the consent of all the parties engaged in the conflict itself. This in large part explains the sudden explosion of UN peace operations in the 1990s.

of disputes remained limited. Since the late 1980s the situation has become even more complicated.

Peacekeeping overreach

The end of the Cold War was followed by a dramatic explosion of UN peacekeeping operations. In 1988–89, for example, five new peacekeeping operations were added, to monitor the Afghanistan/Pakistan border, the Iran-Iraq ceasefire, the end of fighting in Angola's long-lasting civil war, the resolution of Namibia's independence struggle, and the ceasefires between rival factions in Central America. In subsequent years the roster kept growing as Western Sahara, Cambodia, Bosnia-Herzegovina, Somalia, Mozambique, Rwanda, Haiti, and other regions saw the arrival of a UN peace operation.

The slew of new missions required new organizational structures and additional resources, summarized in the UN Secretary-General's Agenda for Peace of January 1992. In the same year, the UN created the Department of Peacekeeping Operations (DPKO) to coordinate the various peace operations. The number of blue-helmeted soldiers jumped from about 15,000 in 1991 to more than 76,000 in 1994. In the same period the financial cost of UN peacekeeping operations grew more than 600 percent, from roughly $490 million in 1991 to $3.3 billion in 1994. Not surprisingly, the human costs went up in a dramatic fashion: there were 15 deaths among UN peacekeepers in 1991 but 252 in 1993 (so far the highest annual casualty rate in the history of UN peacekeeping).

The post–Cold War activism of the UN in peacekeeping did not always produce the desired results. This was, probably, in part due to the complexity of the new missions. In contrast to "classical peacekeeping" between nation-states, the UN peacekeepers were suddenly thrown into a number of civil war situations and effectively mandated to enforce a settlement that may or may

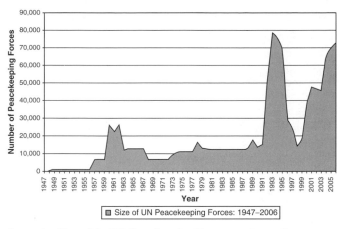

CHART 4.1 Size of the UN Peacekeeping Forces: 1947–2006.

not have had the acquiescence of warring parties. Whether classified as second, third, or fourth generation peace operations, the record of these efforts was, particularly in the early 1990s, mixed.

Some of the successes of UN peacekeeping operations included El Salvador and Mozambique, where UN peacekeepers helped provide the internal security necessary to achieve sustainable peace. The case of El Salvador further contributed to the successful search for peace in Central America that laid the basis for the "democratization" of the region at large. Between 1992 and 1994 just over six thousand peacekeepers of the UN Operation in Mozambique (ONUMOZ) helped oversee that Southeast African nation's transition from a state of civil war to representative democracy. Earlier, in 1989–90, the UN Transition Assistance Group (UNTAG) had managed to guide Namibia from a prolonged independence struggle toward independence. The point, though, was that in the transition phase from the Cold War international system to a post–Cold War one, UN peace operations managed to produce stability in a number of the world's trouble spots.

8. Secretary-General Boutros Boutros-Ghali is escorted by Egyptian peacekeeping troops on a visit to Sarajevo in December 1992.

At approximately the same time, 15,000 UN peacekeepers—as part of the UN Advance Mission in Cambodia (UNAMIC, 1991–92) and the UN Transitional Authority in Cambodia (UNTAC, 1992–93)— oversaw the implementation of the Comprehensive Political Settlement of the Cambodia Conflict (signed in Paris on October 23, 1991). This was a particularly impressive achievement, given that Cambodia had seen more than two decades of continuous civil strife and a genocidal campaign by the Khmer Rouge in the late 1970s that had resulted in the death of more than two million people. Although the UN's record was not perfect, the operations in Cambodia showed the potentially beneficial impact that international organizations could have in transforming a war-torn society into a peaceful one.

It did not matter much, though, that the UN could point to certain successful peace operations in the early 1990s. By the middle of the decade it was clear that the early post–Cold War enthusiasm regarding the UN's role as a global peacekeeper had started to wane. This was largely due to three magnificent failures.

Two of these tragic failures took place in Africa. Between 1992 and 1995, two UN Operations in Somalia (UNOSOM I & II) failed to produce a secure environment in a country split by civil war and ruled by rival militia groups. In 1994 the Rwandan genocide, the massacre of at least 800,000 members of the Tutsi tribe by two extremist Hutu groups between April and July, took place despite the presence of the UN Assistance Mission for Rwanda (UNAMIR). More than a decade after the departure of UNOSOM II and UNAMIR, Somalia and Rwanda remain politically unstable, classic examples of the shortcomings of post–Cold War peace enforcement.

Equally dramatic was the failure of the UN—or any other international force—to prevent the ethnic cleansing in former Yugoslavia. Particularly shocking was the 1995 massacre of an estimated 8,000 Bosniaks (Bosnian Muslims) in Srebrenica, an area declared a "safe haven" by the UN Security Council. But not even a unanimous Security Council resolution, nor the presence of 400 Dutch peacekeepers, could stop the worst massacre in Europe since World War II.

Together with Somalia and Rwanda, Bosnia served to discredit those who had placed high hopes in UN peacekeeping in the post–Cold War era. Thus, after peace agreements (the Dayton Agreements) that were eventually negotiated to end the wars of former Yugoslavia in October 1995, the UNSC did not authorize a UN force to oversee their implementation. Instead, it delegated all military tasks to NATO's Implementation Force (IFOR).

These highly public failures did not completely erase the belief in the positive role of peace operations that had been nurtured by the earlier successes in Central America, Africa, and Asia. And yet, by the mid-1990s, the successes seemed to pale in comparison to some of the magnificent and deadly failures of UN peacekeeping. Stocktaking followed.

Reassessments

The contrast between the peacekeeping operations conducted mainly by a multinational UN force and the massive Persian Gulf operation in 1990–91 headed by U.S. troops was clear. The sheer size of the latter, dubbed Operation Desert Storm, was such that it could not have been conducted by the modest resources available to the UN. Nor would the United States—or a number of other countries—yield its ultimate command over its own national military to some supranational body. The Gulf War may well have been a successful implementation of a UNSC resolution. But because making Iraqi forces retreat from Kuwait was possible *only* through the use of large-scale military force, the Gulf War was more a demonstration of American military might as the lone superpower than an indication of the UN's new robust role in safeguarding international peace and security.

A comparison of the resources put into driving Iraq out of Kuwait with those allocated to the peacekeeping missions in the first five years of the post–Cold War era illustrates the point. At their peak the coalition forces in the Persian Gulf numbered 660,000; estimates of the financial costs of the war range from $61 to $71 billion (an estimated $53 billion came from countries other than the United States, although the Americans committed more than three-quarters of the troops engaged in the conflict).

By contrast, in 1993, the year when the costs of post–Cold War UN peacekeeping peaked, the total budget allocated was $3.6 billion; the total number of blue helmets was just below 80,000 (scattered in thirteen different missions on three different continents). The late 1990s would see a gradual decline in operations as well as the funds devoted to them until the new millennium saw yet another rise in both. The number of peacekeepers breached the 100,000 barrier in summer 2008; the budget had climbed to $5.4 billion.

It is difficult to judge whether peacekeeping missions are adequately funded. It is clear, however, that the UN spends but a minuscule proportion of the national defense spending (roughly 1 percent of the French and less than 0.1 percent of the U.S.) of most major powers. This relatively modest funding may well be one reason why peacekeeping did not ultimately become the great success story of the 1990s. Ironically, however, the growth of peacekeeping costs tends to attract much more attention and criticism than the much higher cost of, say, the first Gulf War.

The so-called Brahimi Report on UN Peace Operations (named after Ambassador Lakhdar Brahimi of Algeria, who had the impressively long title of "Chairman, Under-Secretary-General for Special Assignments in Support of the Secretary-General's Preventive and Peacemaking Efforts") that was released in 2000 laid bare many of the problems. It pointed to the basic reason why the missions in Rwanda, Somalia, and Bosnia had failed: they had not been deployed to post-conflict situations but tried to create a post-conflict environment with inadequate resources. In short, war needed to end before peace could be built, but the UN force lacked the mandate and the resources to enforce a peace.

The Brahimi Report also drew a clear distinction between peacekeepers and peacebuilders, pointing out that the two groups needed to work closely together if sustainable peace were to be forged. To improve the situation, the report went on to list no fewer than twenty key recommendations for UN peace operations. Among these were the need for preventive action, clear and credible mandates for the missions, added funding and logistical support, and an improved public information capacity.

The recommendations lacked the simplicity that would have appealed to political pundits. They were logical and well argued but could never be expected to produce immediate results. They were backed up by Secretary-General Kofi Annan, who called a reform of the UN Peacekeeping Operations essential. Annan

The Brahimi Report, 2000

Officially called the "Report of the Panel on United Nations Peacekeeping Operations," the Brahimi Report gets its name from the chairman of the committee that drafted it, the Algerian diplomat Lakhdar Brahimi, who had previously served as UN envoy to Haiti and South Africa. This report, released in 2000, followed up on the 1992 "Agenda for Peace." The Brahimi Report took a critical view of UN peace operations in the 1990s and provided a list of twenty recommendations. In particular, the report called for extensive restructuring of the Department of Peacekeeping Operations; a new information and strategic analysis unit to service all United Nations departments concerned with peace and security; an integrated task force at Headquarters to plan and support each peacekeeping mission from its inception; and more systematic use of information technology.

In subsequent years, the UN has followed a number of these recommendations by, for example, establishing the Peacebuilding Commission in 2006 and through the establishment of the Secretary-General's High Level Panel on Threats, Challenges and Change, which delivered its report on the future security challenges of the UN in 2004.

further demanded that it was finally time to place peacekeeping at the center of UN activities. To achieve this purpose, however, many more funds were needed. Thus, Annan made a plea to member states to increase their funding for UN peace operations.

The response was positive but incremental and uneven. The expenditures on peacekeeping operations had hovered between $1 billion and $1.5 billion in 1996–99. By 2002–03 the figure had almost doubled; in 2005 the UN spent over $4.7 billion (more than three times as much as a decade earlier). Eighteen operations with about 25,000 peacekeepers in 1997, and twenty-two operations with roughly 70,000 soldiers were active in 2005, respectively.

More peacekeepers did not mean a more peaceful world. If anything, the surge in numbers suggested that there were more trouble spots in the world after, rather than during, the Cold War. More disturbingly, a number of conflict areas remained stubbornly warlike despite lengthy UN involvement. Clearly, UN peacekeepers had proven their worth when it came to separating two hostile nations that saw it in their interest to end hostilities (as in Suez or Cyprus). Clearly UN troops could, in certain contexts, successfully enforce peace inside an internally divided country (as in the Congo). But building a durable peace, a nation that was not at war with itself, was more difficult.

The challenge of peacebuilding

Since the mid-1940s the business of keeping, maintaining, and enforcing peace has been high on the UN's agenda. It remains so today and is likely to continue as long as military conflicts persist—as they unfortunately are likely to do—in the future. Recognizing this fact and the limited successes of peace operations (as spelled out in the Brahimi Report) in general, the UN General Assembly voted to establish the Peacebuilding Commission (PC) in late 2005. The commission held its first meeting in the summer of 2006. Its mission was to "marshal resources at the disposal of the international community to advise and propose integrated strategies for post-conflict recovery, focusing attention on reconstruction, institution-building and sustainable development in countries emerging from conflict."

This was a fine idea. It reflected the fact that in the new millennium the scope for traditional peacekeeping à la Suez post-1956 was obsolete and peace enforcement was possible only under specific conditions—when there was no opposition to such an effort from the UN Security Council's P-5. The 2003 U.S.-led intervention had further demonstrated the incapacity of the UN in keeping a superpower like the United States from using its military might to deadly effect without the UN's blessing. However, the Iraq war's aftermath has showed how crucial a role the UN could potentially play in a post-conflict environment. Traditional peacekeeping was meant to buy time for interstate diplomacy and conflict resolution. The UN's peacebuilders are to buy time for the transition period that followed the many twenty-first-century internal conflicts around the globe.

The founding of the Peacebuilding Commission is a commendable step toward a more nuanced and flexible way of addressing the future of the world's major trouble spots. Yet the commission alone will be able to accomplish little. It is an advisory body, consisting of thirty-one representatives of UN member states (including the P-5). As its website spells out "the Commission's power will come from the quality of its advice and the weight carried by its membership."[3] In other words, it works by consensus and can ultimately do little more than offer advice. It is no miracle cure.

If there is one lesson to be learned from this latest development, it is the fact that there is a continued need for measures that go beyond the simple blocking of two hostile sides from attacking each other. *Keeping* peace may well have been what the first UN peace operations aimed to do, but the far more arduous challenge is the *building* of peace. In order to do this, the Peacebuilding Commission was to "bring together the UN's broad capacities and experience in conflict prevention, mediation, peacekeeping, respect for human rights, the rule of law, humanitarian assistance, reconstruction and long-term development."

Peacebuilding is, therefore, a holistic exercise that recognizes both the significance of the UN's economic role as well as contributions of the various well-known humanitarian organizations that together form the "softer side" of the United Nations.

Chapter 5
Economic development to human development

The UN Charter drew a link between international security and global poverty. The founders believed that World War II was in large measure an outcome of the Great Depression of the 1930s; in other words, that economic turmoil had been transformed into political instability, which in turn was a precondition to the Nazi takeover in Germany. One of the UN's central goals was to prevent similar economic upheaval and the political consequences that derived from it. The founders—at least some of them—hoped to head off economic collapse, war, and revolution by a dose of social democratic reforms and intergovernmental policy coordination.

But while the UN Charter speaks of promoting "higher standards of living" and creating "conditions of economic and social progress and development," there has never been an agreement on *how* these goals should be advanced. In the early postwar years the major issue on the agenda was the recovery of Western Europe and Japan. In the 1950s and 1960s the process of decolonization and the emergence of the so-called Third World shifted the focus toward questions of global inequality. Although international relations may have been guided by the East-West conflict, the persistent North-South divide overshadowed the UN's efforts to reshape the global economy.

And so it remained when, in September 2000, the General Assembly adopted the Millennium Development Goals (MDGs). The UN's major task was to make the world a better place by, among other things, eradicating poverty and hunger, achieving universal education, empowering women, and fighting infant mortality. None of these extremely worthy goals was new. All remain "goals" today.

Yet, as Miguel A. Albornoz, the Ecuadorian ambassador to the UN, succinctly put it in a speech at the UN General Assembly in 1985: "In the developing countries the United Nations doesn't mean frustration, confrontation or condemnation. It means environmental sanitation, agricultural production, tele-communications, the fight against illiteracy, the great struggle against poverty, ignorance and disease."[1] In spite of its problems and in the minds of many at the receiving end, the UN has done more than any other organization or single nation to alleviate the economic and social problems of the less developed countries. It is a story that—however imperfect the end results—cannot be ignored in putting the UN's economic activities in perspective.

Reconstruction after World War II

In 1945 Europe was in ruins. Most ancient capitals were physically crumbling, unemployment was at record high levels, millions of refugees were displaced, and famine loomed. In Asia, Japan and China were both reeling from the physical destruction caused by a war that had, for all intents and purposes, begun in 1937. In China a civil war continued until the formation of the People's Republic of China on October 1, 1949.

The only major exception in the bleak picture was the United States, a country that produced half of the world's industrial goods in 1945. Thus it was no accident that the Americans shaped the postwar world. Yet, because of the simultaneous descent into the Cold War, the economic reconstruction of most of the globe became excessively politicized. From 1948 to 1952 the Marshall Plan—or the European Recovery Program (ERP)—benefited only Western Europe, the Soviet Union having pressured the eastern half to stay out of such schemes. The fear of losing control over its new satellite countries in East-Central Europe made the Kremlin particularly antagonistic to any economic or political scheme that might have helped vest the region from Soviet control.

In the Far East, especially after 1947, the United States gave generous reconstruction assistance to Japan. In both cases the major rationale behind U.S. policy was to prevent a potential left-wing drift of the countries that became its major Cold War allies. Meanwhile, the Soviet Union tied Eastern European countries closely to its economic and political orbit. The end result was, in effect, the creation of what would later be referred to as the "first world" (North America, Western Europe, and Japan) and the "second world" (the Soviet Union and its satellites in Europe).

Postwar reconstruction aid was significant in the creation of this new economic world order. But it was a fleeting phase, deriving mainly from immediate political and security concerns. Much like NATO in the security field, the Marshall Plan served to tie the major European countries to the United States economically. The side effect—and an intended one—of these efforts was to erect a barrier between what would soon be called propagandistically the "free world" and the parts of the world that lived under the influence of Soviet communism.

This also meant, however, that one of the charter's main ideas, the world body's commitment to "economic and social progress and development," was essentially a casualty of the political division of the world after 1945. Of course, no one openly disputed the need for economic progress. But the instruments by which it could be promoted were controversial. Specifically, the first and second worlds had their own ideas about how to promote economic and social progress. The Americans emphasized free trade and the role of the private sector; the Soviets heralded the salutary effects of government control and refused to join in the global trade network. Although in 1944–45 many Americans thought that governments and businesses should cooperate closely in postwar reconstruction efforts, they saw this as at best a temporary phenomenon. During the Cold War this Soviet-American, socialist-capitalist dichotomy laid a shadow over the UN's role in promoting development and reducing poverty.

Trade and growth

The UN's economic agenda was originally controlled by the so-called Bretton Woods institutions, named after the city in New Hampshire where, in July 1944, representatives of forty-three countries met to contemplate the postwar international economic order. The three key institutions of this system are still operational and influential today: the International Monetary Fund (IMF), the World Bank (originally called the International Bank for Reconstruction and Development, or IBRD), and the World Trade Organization (WTO, known as the General Agreement on Tariffs and Trade, or GATT, between 1947 and 1995). All three reflected a certain ideological view on how the international economy should function: while the GATT/WTO developed into an institution upholding the principle of ever-freer trading rules (if not always successfully), the IMF was set up to increase stability in the world's currency market, and the IBRD/World Bank was to provide financial assistance to countries willing but otherwise unable to join the world market.

These were institutions conceived to prop up, expand, and regulate the global marketplace. They were, by and large, Anglo-American in their design. The World Bank, for example, received approximately 35 percent of its original $9.1 billion capitalization from the United States. Moreover, it is important to note that the World Bank and the IMF in particular were founded as organizations in which the power lay with those who paid. In other words, the voting power in these organizations was skewed to the rich and powerful countries (the major contributors), with the United States at the top. While the United States and other rich Western nations were undoubtedly concerned over economic stability and security, their agenda was dominated by the belief that the promotion of free trade through international treaties and mechanisms was the best guarantee against future international economic collapse and offered the best hope of future prosperity around the globe.

It is a mantra that has had its success. Since 1945 international trade has grown rapidly in volume and contributed greatly to the growth of global gross and per capita income. Between 1960 and 1993, for example, global income grew from $4 trillion to $23 trillion. Even when adjusted to global population growth, this still meant a threefold increase of per capita income.

This apparent success story had its critics and opponents. The U.S.-funded Marshall Plan was rejected by the USSR in 1947 and followed by the creation of a socialist economic system within the Soviet bloc. Equally adamantly, after 1949 the People's Republic of China rejected capitalism as a way of promoting "economic and social advancement." In the decades that followed, the IMF, World Bank, and GATT remained "Western" institutions promoting one side's vision in the global confrontation. In the late 1980s and early 1990s, the end of the Cold War seemingly proved that the Western vision had been correct and the socialist way erroneous. The disintegration of the USSR underlined this point.

The second challenge came from decolonization. The explosive growth in membership transformed the balance of power within the UN General Assembly: during the early 1960s the Nonaligned Movement (NAM) emerged as the largest—if a very loosely coordinated—group of countries. This shift resulted in a growing emphasis on social and economic questions, particularly on the unequal distribution of wealth between the countries of the global

North and South. The first UN Conference on Trade and Development (UNCTAD) held in 1964 highlighted this by the formation of the Group of 77 (G-77), an organization of developing countries in Latin America, Asia, and Africa that continues to promote the importance of development aid.

By 2008 the G-77 comprised more than 130 countries in the so-called global South. Most of them are poor and underdeveloped compared to Europe and North America. But their sheer numbers, both countries and people within them, and the persistent fact of global economic inequality have presented a continuous challenge to the UN system.

Development tops the agenda
The World Bank and IDA

In the 1960s the UN's economic agenda shifted from reconstruction to development. The World Bank rapidly became an institution focusing on development aid. In 1960 it founded a subsidiary, the International Development Association (IDA). While the original World Bank lending agency, the IBRD, had shifted its focus to so-called middle-income countries, the IDA's task was to provide interest-free loans and grants to the least developed ones, countries that already in the 1950s were called the "third world."

The first IDA loans, to Chile, Honduras, India, and Sudan, were approved in 1961. Over the subsequent forty-five years the IDA gave roughly $161 billion in loans (usually called credits) to 108 countries. Most of them have gone to Africa; in 2008 half were in sub-Saharan Africa.

Despite such apparent good intentions, the IDA was often resented by those in the receiving end. The World Bank is an institution controlled by those who fund its operations. Thus, the United States as the primary "shareholder" has dominant influence over the bank's priorities. This fact is further underlined by the agreement to have an American president of the World Bank and to station the headquarters of the organization, as well as the IMF, in Washington. Controversial choices for this post—such as former U.S. secretary of defense Robert McNamara (1968–81) or Assistant Secretary of Defense Paul Wolfowitz (2005–07)—have not helped the World Bank's overall reputation. Indeed, many southern countries have seen the World Bank as a renewed form of Western (or Northern) imperialism. Thus, since the 1960s there has been a push for alternative ways of promoting development within the UN system.

UNCTAD

One significant expression of this desire was the first meeting of UNCTAD, held in 1964 in Geneva. It had two significant long-term results. First, it led to the creation of the Group of 77 as a powerful lobby for the interests of developing countries. Second, over the past four decades, UNCTAD has taken the integration of developing countries into the world economy as its key mission.

In the 1960s and 1970s UNCTAD emerged as a key forum for the dialogue between North and South (or developed and developing countries) and as the major global think tank on development issues. It was instrumental in pushing through international agreements that gave developing countries improved market access through lower tariffs in developed countries. UNCTAD further contributed to defining how much developed countries should devote to development aid (in 1970, UNGA approved 0.7 percent of gross domestic product as a target figure) and identified a group of nations defined as Least Developed Countries (LDCs, sometimes called the "fourth world").

UNCTAD is important in setting the course of the UN's development policy. But even by UN standards it remains a small operation. After more than four decades in operation, UNCTAD has a permanent staff of about four hundred (mostly in Geneva) and an annual regular budget of $50 million. It gives advice, prepares data, offers technical assistance, and organizes a major conference every four years (and a conference focusing on the needs of the LDCs every ten years). UNCTAD lobbies and coordinates, but it does not make policy.

UNDP

The creation of the UN Development Program (UNDP) in 1965 was a milestone in global development policy. Its initial purpose was to coordinate the Expanded Programme of Technical Assistance (EPTA) and the United Nations Special Fund (UNSF), operational since 1949 and 1959 respectively, in order to respond better to the needs of a growing number of newly independent countries.

In subsequent decades the UNDP, which depends on voluntary contributions from member countries, has become an increasingly important part of the UN. One indication of this is the fact that the UNDP's administrator, or chief executive officer, formally ranks as number three in the UN structure after the Secretary-General and the Deputy Secretary-General. In this regard, however, the UNDP hardly became symbolic of the third world's hope of circumventing the rich nations' dominance of development aid: much like the World Bank, the UNDP has been mostly governed by an American. The appointment of the Briton Mark Malloch Brown in 1999 finally broke this pattern; he was succeeded in 2005 by Kemal Dervis, former Minister for Economic Affairs of Turkey.

UNDP and its predecessors began as institutions offering technical aid (training) and global think tanks producing feasibility studies. But over the decades, UN development aid has become a multi-billion-dollar global enterprise. By 1989 contributions to the UNDP totaled $1.1 billion. It had a staff of 4,700, more than 130 field offices, and worked in 152 countries and territories. Less than two decades later the budget had more than quadrupled to roughly $4.5 billion (2005 figure). Impressive, yet it leaves UNDP far behind the World Bank, which loaned close to $30 billion and boasted a staff of more than eight thousand in the same year.

These are large figures. And it is clear that by 1990 there had already been a great deal of progress. Some of the highlights were summarized by the UNDP as follows:

- from 1960 to 1987, life expectancy in the global South had increased by a third (although it still remained only 80 percent when compared to the developed countries)

- from 1970 to 1985, access to education in the South had dramatically improved; for example, literacy rates had gone up from 43 percent to 60 percent in the South

- from 1965 to 1980, average per capita income had gone up by almost 3 percent every year in developing nations

- from 1960 to 1988, child mortality rates were halved

In short, as the international system underwent the transformation from the cold-war years to a new era, there appeared to be plenty of reason for optimism. Already, the global South had seen a creation of "conditions of economic and social progress." With the ideological rivalries between East and West over, the search for regional proxies through military assistance seemed to give way for various peacekeeping and peacebuilding operations in the world's conflict areas. The era of globalization sent global growth rates soaring in the 1990s. Although it may not have played a major role in prompting such changes, the UNDP could, with certain justification, feel confident that it was "time to put people back at the center of the development process in terms of economic debate, policy and advocacy,"[2] as the UNDP's first *Human Development Report* (*HDR*), published in 1990, put it.

Globalization and human development

The UNDP's confidence reflected a long overdue paradigm shift. Instead of looking at such plain statistics as the growth of a country's GNP or the average income levels in various nations, the

HDR wanted to "assess the level of people's long-term well-being." Thus, such indicators as life expectancy, education, health, nutrition, sanitation, and gender discrimination were considered equally, if not more, important in assessing where a given country ranked in the Human Development Index (HDI). The index was developed in 1990 by Pakistani economist Mahbub ul Haq and has been used in the HDRs since 1993.

The goal of the HDRs and HDIs was to discover how development policies affected average people's daily lives. The reports were then to be used to improve policies and assure that the circle of development beneficiaries was extended. In simple terms, the sheer accumulation of wealth and assets was merely one among many indicators used to assess human development.

The first HDR was, in fact, rather depressing reading. Among other things, in 1990:

- average life expectancy in the South remained twelve years shorter than in the North
- 100 million primary-school age children could not attend school in the South
- 900 million adults were illiterate (in South Asia overall literacy rate was only 41 percent); female literacy rates were roughly two-thirds that of males
- in the 1980s per capita income declined by 2.4 percent in sub-Saharan Africa
- 14 million children died every year before their fifth birthday
- 3 billion people (roughly half of the world's population) lived without proper sanitation

There were, obviously, plenty of challenges for the future and plenty of work for the various specialized UN agencies. UNDP itself could coordinate some of it, yet others—the World Health Organization (WHO), the UN Children's Fund (UNICEF), the

Food and Agriculture Organization (FAO), the World Food
Program (WFP), and the UN Educational, Scientific, and Cultural
Organization (UNESCO) among others—were often better fitted
to meeting many of the specific challenges. Thus, in 1994
Secretary-General Boutros Boutros-Ghali issued "An Agenda for
Development" that emphasized the need for coordination across
UN agencies through UNDP resident coordinators that would be
guided by specific "country strategy notes." Upon unveiling the
paper, however, Boutros-Ghali sounded a warning note:

> At present the UN mechanism is caught in a confining cycle. There is
> a resistance to multilateralism from those who fear a loss of national
> control. There is a reluctance to provide financial means to achieve
> agreed ends from those who lack conviction that assessments will
> benefit their own interests. And there is an unwillingness to engage
> in difficult operations by those who seek guarantees of perfect clarity
> and limited duration. Without a new and compelling collective
> vision, the international community will be unable to break out of
> this cycle.[3]

Unfortunately, by the late 1990s it was clear that the "Agenda for
Development" had failed in providing such a "new and compelling
collective vision." Most significantly, human development was
proceeding on an inequitable basis. Western Europe, North
America, Australia, and Japan ranked high on the Human
Development Index, while Africa, especially sub-Saharan Africa,
was lagging even farther behind than a decade earlier. Indeed, the
1999 HDR, subtitled "Globalization with a Human Face," asserted
that "the top fifth of the world's people in the richest countries
enjoy 82% of the expanding export trade and 68% of foreign direct
investment—the bottom fifth, barely more than 1%."[4]

Millennium Development Goals (MDGs)

The inequalities of the globalized world prompted the UN General
Assembly to publicize an ambitious development agenda for the

Millennium Development Goals, September 2000

The Millennium Development Goals (MDGs) are a long- and medium-term (2000–15) development agenda unveiled by UN Secretary-General Kofi Annan and approved by the General Assembly. The eight MDGs are:

Goal 1 Eradicate extreme poverty and hunger
Goal 2 Achieve universal primary education
Goal 3 Promote gender equality and empower women
Goal 4 Reduce child mortality
Goal 5 Improve maternal health
Goal 6 Combat HIV/AIDS, malaria, and other diseases
Goal 7 Ensure environmental sustainability
Goal 8 Develop a global partnership for development

new century. The eight Millennium Development Goals (MDGs) of September 18, 2000, set 2015 as a target date for, among other things, halving extreme poverty, halting the spread of HIV/AIDS, and providing universal primary education. In short, the MDGs—a result of a plethora of international conference activity in the second half the 1990s—were concerned mainly with lifting the poorest of the poorest (the LDCs) from their wretched state. By 2000 this meant that much of the focus of MDG activity was to be in Africa.

The adoption of the MDGs was a potential turning point in UN development efforts. Finally, there was a blueprint of "only" eight goals, accompanied by a timeline. Yet problems were evident from the beginning. For one, little had changed in terms of those who grant aid (the wealthy nations) and those who receive it (the poor ones). This implied a clear hierarchy and a continued dependency by the South on the goodwill of the North. It also points to one eternal question of development aid: Should aid be conditional on the recipient country's good behavior (or "good governance," as defined by the donor countries)? Or is setting such preconditions an affront to one of the shining principles of the UN Charter: national self-determination?

Another difficulty was that the MDGs suffered from a typical UN syndrome: trying to offer something for every interest group. The eight MDGs were broken down to eighteen "quantifiable targets" (for example, "1. Reduce by half the proportion of people living on less than a dollar a day"). These were to be measured by forty-eight "indicators" (for example, the number of people living on less than $1 per day). But as even these examples suggest, neither the targets nor the indicators were easily agreed upon. There has been a constant debate about whether "dollar-a-day" is an acceptable poverty benchmark to be used when classifying people who live in "extreme poverty" (as opposed to "just" poverty). That the figure is one used by the World Bank does not satisfy the many critics of that institution. But neither does it mean that the various organizations within the UN system that engage in development work make no difference.

The softer side of development: UNICEF

In December 1946 the General Assembly created what remains probably the most widely admired UN agency, the UN International Children's Emergency Fund (or UNICEF; although the name would later be shortened to the UN Children's Fund, the acronym remained, thankfully, the same). Based in New York, UNICEF is intended to provide humanitarian and developmental assistance to children and their mothers, mainly in the developing world.

UNICEF's first mission was to ease the suffering in postwar Europe. Between 1946 and 1950 UNICEF distributed clothes to five million children, vaccinated eight million against tuberculosis, and provided supplemental meals to millions of children. European recovery was undoubtedly eased by these efforts.

9. A UNICEF doctor applies ointment to a child's eye to treat trachoma, a highly contagious disease.

Starting in the 1950s, however, UNICEF expanded its operations to other parts of the globe and became increasingly active in the decolonized world. Health campaigns, including large-scale vaccination projects (against malaria, yaws, leprosy), remained central to the organization's program.

At the same time as UNDP emerged as the UN's development arm, UNICEF was transformed from a short-term emergency agency into a long-term developmental one. While it continued to meet emergency needs of children caught in conflict areas or rendered homeless by natural disasters, UNICEF moved into the long-range benefit approach. To raise nutritional standards for children, UNICEF helped countries produce and distribute low-cost, high-protein foods, and fostered programs to educate people in their use. To provide for the social welfare of children, UNICEF instituted informal training of mothers in child rearing and home improvement, and aided services for children through day care and neighborhood centers, family counseling, and youth clubs.

In later decades, UNICEF further broadened its policy by adopting the so-called country approach. This meant allying aid for children to the development of the (in most cases newly independent) nation. Consequently, UNICEF became concerned with the intellectual, psychological, and vocational needs of children as well as with their physical needs. This meant that UNICEF began, among other things, providing assistance for teacher education and curriculum reform in developing countries. In sum, UNICEF may have been founded as an agency concerned with meeting the immediate needs of suffering children. Over the years, however, its mission—reflecting the changes in the composition of the UN itself—was broadened and aligned with the broader development agenda of the world organization.

In the twenty-first century UNICEF remains most people's favorite UN agency. It has offices in more than 120 countries and staff working in the field in more than 150. Its expenditures are approximately $1.6 billion, funded from voluntary contributions. Among the UN's special funds, programs, and specialized agencies, only the World Food Program (WFP)—often working in close partnership with UNICEF—has a larger budget.

Although it is difficult to assess the exact impact of UNICEF's many programs on developing countries, it is safe to say that the organization has helped millions of children to grow up healthier, safer, and better educated. Some statistics may help in grasping this achievement. For example, in the first twenty-five years of its existence UNICEF vaccinated 400 million children against tuberculosis; helped set up 12,000 rural health centers and several thousand maternity wards in eighty-five countries; provided equipment for 2,500 teacher training schools and 56,000 primary and secondary schools; and supplied billions of supplementary meals. In 1965 UNICEF was, deservedly, awarded the Nobel Peace Prize for making a positive difference in the lives of millions of children.

Paying (or not) for development

Money—where it comes from and where it goes to—has always been a controversial issue in UN development policy. Yet, since the late 1960s there has been a surprising unanimity of opinion concerning how much wealthier countries should devote to helping the less fortunate ones: at least 0.7 percent of their gross national income (GNI). Unfortunately, there has also been a virtually unanimous inability to meet that goal.

The figure is based on a report commissioned by World Bank president (and former U.S. secretary of defense) Robert S. McNamara in 1968, the first year that had actually witnessed a decline in development aid. The Commission on International Development was headed by former Canadian prime minister Lester Pearson, who had won the Nobel Peace Prize for his role in the creation of the first large peacekeeping force following the Suez crisis in 1956. The Pearson Commission had seven other members, who, with the exception of a Brazilian representative, all came from the developed world. They delivered their final report (called "Partners in Development") on September 15, 1969.

The report's basic point was that a "much-increased flow of aid will be required if most developing countries are to aim for self-sustaining growth by the end of the century." The Pearson report set two targets for donor countries: while official (government) development assistance (ODA) should be 0.7 percent of the country's GNI, total aid (including private sources) should amount to 1 percent of GNI. The target date for reaching this ODA/GNI ratio was 1975.

Three decades later, and despite repeated agreements and commitments to the contrary—usually made at world summits organized by the UN or one of its agencies—only five countries were meeting this seemingly modest goal. But however much these small, wealthy nations—Denmark, Luxembourg, Netherlands,

Norway, Sweden—spend on ODA, their relative contribution will always be modest. Indeed, the United States remains the world's largest single aid donor, followed by Japan, the United Kingdom, France, and Germany. Remarkably, of the five top donors only the UK's ODA/GNI percentage rose between 1990 and 2004. The collective ODA/GNI ratio for the wealthiest twenty-two countries in the world was 0.33 percent in 2005, less than half of the 1975 goal set by Pearson and his colleagues.

It should be noted that in actual monetary terms development aid has increased substantially: from about $7 billion in the late 1960s to $106 billion in 2005. But given the explosion of global income and the fact that its primary beneficiaries have been the developed countries, the proportion these countries actually spend on development aid has declined.

One last, less than encouraging statistic is worth mentioning. Following the wide publicity given to the MDGs and in particular the sudden flow of aid to such war-torn countries as Afghanistan and Iraq after 2001, development aid grew substantially in the first five years of the new millennium. But in 2006 it declined by about 5.1 percent when compared to the year before; it was expected to do the same in 2007. The trend is widely assumed to continue.

Failing to meet the UN's ODA targets is, of course, only part of the story. There is no guarantee that even if all the richer countries in the world actually met the 0.7 percent ratio, the money would be well spent. It would depend on the conditions at the receiving end, on the appropriate allocation of the resources available.

The major point, however, is not that the task of development is entirely and necessarily hopeless. Rather, the point is that so far the ones who "have"—the developed nations—have not met the targets they have set for *themselves* when designing the means for helping those who "have not."

Development in crisis

In 2007 the UNDP's website proclaimed that it is "on the ground in 166 countries, working with them on their own solutions to global and national development challenges ... UNDP seeks to ensure the most effective use of UN and international aid resources."

This declaration may sound impressive, but simple arithmetic is helpful in putting this into perspective. Deduct from the total number seven liaison offices in highly developed countries (Canada, Denmark, France, Japan, Netherlands, Norway, and Sweden). Then ask yourself why the remaining 159 (representing 83 percent of the 192 UN member countries) need a UNDP mission. Something, it seems, has not been working as planned when it comes down to economic and social development. Despite fervent activity, numerous plans and initiatives, the involvement of dozens of organizations and institutions, economic and social development remains lopsided with the world divided into the haves and the have nots more or less along the same geographic lines as in the 1960s.

Of course, not everything has gone wrong; there has been movement. A brief look at progress in trying to reach the MDGs provides a rather more complex picture of development policies and their impact. In April 2007, for example, the World Bank's Global Monitoring Report confidently pronounced that "the world as a whole will meet MDG 1 of halving poverty" by 2015. But while there was evidence that both "extreme poverty" (the number of people living on less than $1 per day) and "poverty" (people who live on less than $2 per day) rates had declined, such progress was widely uneven. While North Africa, the Middle East, and the Far East were "on target," Latin America, the Caribbean, and Central Asia were lagging behind. Worst off was sub-Saharan Africa, described as "way off target and unlikely to meet" the target of halving extreme poverty by 2015.

Fragile states in 2005 according to the World Bank

The following 35 states and territories were defined as "fragile"—weak institutions and policies, often as a result of lengthy military conflicts—in 2005 (note the absence of Iraq from the list): Afghanistan, Angola, Burundi, Cambodia, Central African Republic, Chad, Comoros, Democratic Republic of Congo, Republic of Congo, Cote d'Ivoire, Djibouti, Eritrea, The Gambia, Guinea, Guinea-Bissau, Haiti, Kosovo, Lao PDR, Liberia, Mauritania, Myanmar, Nigeria, Papua New Guinea, Sao Tome & Principe, Sierra Leone, Solomon Islands, Somalia, Sudan, Timor-Leste, Togo, Tonga, Uzbekistan, Vanuatu, West Bank and Gaza, and Zimbabwe.

The story is very similar regarding a number of the other MDGs. While most regions had made progress in reducing child mortality rates (MDG 4), some were "lagging," with sub-Saharan Africa again being the worst off. In fact, only 32 out of 147 countries were "on track" in halving child mortality by 2015. This was in large part due to poor nutrition—a problem that the rapid rise in global food prices in 2008 could only exacerbate. Depressingly, the World Bank Report noted that almost every developing region had countries making little or no progress in this area (with South Asia and, yes, sub-Saharan Africa again ranking lowest). Of the 35 countries identified by the World Bank as "fragile states"—with weak institutions and policies, often as a result of lengthy military conflicts—the largest proportion were in sub-Saharan Africa.

The statistics, of course, tell us relatively little about the realities that the various aid agencies face in their work. Nor do they give us anything approaching a satisfactory view of what the specific measurements actually mean—surely living on $1 per day in Bangladesh means something different than trying to survive on the same amount in Afghanistan (imagine trying to do the same in Switzerland or the United States). Moreover, they hardly explain what is, or might in the future be, working. But they do seem to indicate that progress is possible and—lest one take a truly cynical view—desirable.

Chapter 6

Rights and responsibilities: human rights to human security

Among the plethora of issues on the UN's agenda, few can be considered more important and challenging than the protection of individual human rights. But making sure that people can live in "freedom from fear," as Secretary-General Dag Hammarskjöld summed up his philosophy of human rights in 1956, is not such a straightforward task as it may appear.[1] The basic problem is simple: the major violators of human rights tend to be states, and states are the major entities that make up the UN.

The central question is this: Is it more important to protect the integrity of a state or the individual being harassed by that state? From that question flow various others, such as: What about those people rendered stateless by violent conflict or ecological disaster? What about people's right to move within and between nation-states?

Based on historical experience, the answer to the key question has often been somewhat unsatisfying. Protection of human rights, much like the general respect for them, has a contingent quality. The state—regardless of its nature (democratic, authoritarian, totalitarian)—has tended to reign supreme over the individual.

The canon: the International Bill of Rights

Human rights were a central issue at the very founding of the UN. Two mileposts from the 1940s established the UN's human rights agenda: In December 1946, the first meeting of the Economic and Social Council (ECOSOC) established the UN Commission on Human Rights (UNCHR). One of its key members was Eleanor Roosevelt, the former First Lady of the United States. It was in large part due to her persistence that exactly two years later the General Assembly issued the Universal Declaration of Human Rights, a document that would later be considered a central part of the so-called International Bill of Rights. Upon submitting the text of the declaration to the UN General Assembly in 1948, Roosevelt spoke eloquently:

> We stand today at the threshold of a great event both in the life of the
> United Nations and in the life of mankind. This declaration may
> well become the international Magna Carta for all men everywhere.
> We hope its proclamation by the General Assembly will be an event
> comparable to the proclamation in 1789 [of the French Declaration
> of the Rights of Man], the adoption of the Bill of Rights by the
> people of the United States, and the adoption of comparable
> declarations at different times in other countries.[2]

The 1948 declaration was based on a simple notion: the "inherent dignity" of all human beings. It linked human rights with international security by maintaining that the respect for human rights "was the foundation of freedom, justice, and peace in our world." The declaration further specified a number of the most obvious violations of human rights, such as slavery and denial of the right to freedom of expression. The document revealed a certain Western bias when it stressed the equal rights of men *and* women. But it also stretched the concept of human rights to include, among others, the right to free education, "equal pay for equal work," and the "right to rest and leisure."

10. Chairman Eleanor Roosevelt speaks at the first meeting of the committee charged by the Commission on Human Rights, Economic and Social Council with drafting the International Bill of Rights in 1947.

Among the tasks of UNCHR was to develop additional international human rights legislation that would add specificity and muscle to the Universal Declaration. In 1966 this work led to the adoption by the General Assembly of two additional human rights covenants: the International Covenant on Civil and Political Rights, and the International Covenant on Economic, Social and Cultural Rights. As their names suggest, the two covenants focused on different aspects of the original 1948 Declaration.

Together the 1948 declaration and the two covenants of 1966 are known as the International Bill of Human Rights. They are undoubtedly a significant, almost revolutionary, achievement. By the mid-1960s there existed a series of universally approved principles that protected men and women against almost any possible—civil, political, economic, or social—form of discrimination and abuse.

The lengthy list of rights does suggest a number of practical problems. Perhaps most important, the list seems ill-suited to a

The International Bill of Human Rights

To supplement the Universal Declaration of Human Rights (1948), the UN General Assembly approved two additional covenants in 1966. Together, these documents comprise the basic canon of human rights today.

1. International Covenant on Civil and Political Rights "include the rights to life, liberty, security of the person, privacy and property; the right to marry and found a family; the right to a fair trial; freedom from slavery, torture and right to a nationality; freedom of thought, conscience and relation; freedom of opinion and expression; freedom of assembly and association; and the right to free elections, universal suffrage and participation in public affairs."

2. International Covenant on Economic, Social and Cultural Rights "include the right to work and a just reward; the right to form and join trade unions; the right to rest and leisure; and to periodic holidays with pay; the right to a standard of living adequate to health and well-being; the right to social security; the right to education; and the right to participation in the cultural life of a community."

world of nation-states, especially one loaded with nondemocratic nations. Indeed, the enforcement of the International Bill of Rights has not been spectacularly successful.

The practice: commissions, rapporteurs and the advance of human rights

In its six decades of existence, the UNCHR went through several stages of development that tended to mirror the overall changes of the UN. In its first two decades the commission focused on the general promotion of human rights but not on condemning violations thereof. The policy was, appropriately, called "absenteeism" and was justified by the UN Charter's strict adherence to the principle of national sovereignty. More than that, a UN resolution of 1947 explicitly stated that the commission "had no power to take any action in regard to any complaints concerning human rights." Petitioning the commission was, in other words, pointless.

Many violators—including both the Soviet Union (with its treatment of any political opposition) and the United States (with the institutionalized racism that was prevalent in the southern states)—were let off the hook. When pleas and petitions arrived, the commission could only state that it had "no competence" to investigate them, much less bring any perpetrators to justice. The UNCHR's authority as an impartial judge of the observance of human rights was therefore damaged from the beginning.

In the mid-1960s the UNCHR moved toward a much more interventionist approach. Part of the reason for the change was the adoption of the International Bill of Rights in 1966. But the other driving force behind the shift was the increase in the number of African states that called upon the UN to condemn apartheid in South Africa. Cold War rivalry over the allegiance of these new states meant that the Soviets and the Americans would not openly object to the new human rights agenda. The UNCHR was thus made "competent": it was given the power to take unilateral action in the case of gross human rights violations. A forum for the discussion of severe human rights abuses with target countries was established.

Accordingly, in the 1970s and 1980s the commission's reach expanded. It was given an indirect boost by the 1975 Conference on Security and Cooperation in Europe (CSCE) that drew a link between human rights and international security (albeit only in the context of Europe). New regional (and even country-specific) and thematic working groups (for example, on minorities or torture) were formed to allow for the in-depth investigation into human rights abuses. A number of Special Rapporteurs were sent out on fact-finding missions to report on specific cases. As a result of such actions, the reporting on human rights violations certainly improved.

UN Special Rapporteurs have a specific mandate (normally for three years) to investigate, monitor, and recommend solutions to human rights problems. They often conduct fact-finding missions to countries to investigate allegations of human rights violations. But they can visit only those countries that have invited them. Rapporteurs also assess complaints from alleged victims of human rights violations. In 2007 there were more than thirty Special Rapporteurs, who could be divided into two groups: those

UN Special Rapporteurs

UN Special Rapporteurs have a specific mandate (normally for three years) to investigate, monitor, and recommend solutions to human rights problems. They often conduct fact-finding missions to countries to investigate allegations of human rights violations. But they can only visit countries that have invited them. Rapporteurs also assess complaints from alleged victims of human rights violations.

The Rapporteurs have no legal powers and cannot take action against governments. They can lobby a government and urge it to respect human rights. They can also raise negative publicity by issuing press statements. Their effectiveness is, as a result, highly suspect and contingent.

In 2007 there were more than thirty Special Rapporteurs that could be divided into two groups, those concerned with specific countries (Belarus, Cambodia, Cuba, North Korea, Sudan, and others) and those who held thematic mandates from the Human Rights Council (Right to Education, Freedom of Religion, Racism, Sale of Children, etc.).

concerned with specific countries (Belarus, Cambodia, Cuba, North Korea, Sudan, and others), and those who held thematic mandates from the Human Rights Council (Right to Education, Freedom of Religion, Racism, Sale of Children, and so forth).

The enforcement capabilities of the Rapporteurs are limited. They have no legal powers and cannot take action against governments. They can lobby a government and urge it to respect human rights. They can also raise negative publicity by issuing press statements. Their effectiveness is, as a result, highly suspect and contingent. For example, the presence of a Special Rapporteur on Myanmar since 1992 has done nothing to quell the dictatorial conduct of that country's military junta. If anything, Myanmar's leadership engaged in some of the most brutal repression in the fall of 2007 and continued to keep the leader of the battered opposition, Aung San Suu Kyi, under house arrest (a status she has "enjoyed" since the late 1980s). A military government, such as Myanmar's, bent on ignoring external opinion, is highly unlikely to change its conduct on the basis of criticism from the UN.

Nevertheless, the overall respect for human rights—in the form of democratization—made rapid advances in the 1980s, culminating in the collapse of the totalitarian order in Eastern Europe and the Soviet Union in 1989–91, the end of apartheid in South Africa, and democratic reforms in a number of Latin American countries. Even as violations did continue—most spectacularly in the form of the 1989 Chinese government's crackdown on student protesters in Beijing's Tiananmen Square—the International Bill of Rights was finally being taken seriously around the globe.

The role of the UNCHR in the process was not necessarily evident, however. It had allowed the most flagrant cases of human rights abuses to go unnoticed. In the People's Republic of China (PRC), Mao Zedong's Great Leap Forward in the 1950s had caused the deaths of millions (some argue thirty million) of his countrymen; that not being enough, Mao engineered another widespread terror campaign in the late 1960s known as the Cultural Revolution. As "punishment" the PRC took Taiwan's seat in the UN and became a permanent member of the Security Council in 1971. Other cases that went virtually unnoticed included the Soviet and Warsaw Pact crackdowns in East Germany (1953), Hungary (1956), and Czechoslovakia (1968). In Cambodia, the Khmer Rouge managed to kill millions (one-eighth of the country's population) in the late 1970s until it was deposed following an invasion by another consistent violator of human rights, Vietnam. Democratization and the growing respect for human rights that accompanied it was as much, if not more, the result of the shifting international environment—the collapse of the cold war international order—than the increased activity of the UN in the field.

In fact, by the 1990s the Human Rights Commission had lost much of its status as a potentially effective guardian of human rights. There were many reasons for this. The Special Rapporteurs, as we read earlier, could visit only those countries that invited them; a major violator was unlikely to do so. The commission itself consisted of fifty-three members, many of them representing countries that were committing—or were implicated in committing—human rights violations (such as the People's Republic of China, Algeria, and Syria).

The central problem that emerged and remains can be summarized as follows. The UNCHR was supposed to stand above the interests of nation-states and render impartial judgment based upon broadly accepted certain legal standards. But over the years, the commission became excessively politicized and was, in the end, unable to fulfill its mission effectively during the Cold War era. By the early 1990s it had lost much of its credibility.

The response to such concerns was in some ways a typical UN one: they organized and held a big conference. The World Conference on Human Rights, which had been first proposed by the General Assembly in 1989, finally met in the summer of 1993 in Vienna.

It brought together representatives from 171 countries and 800 NGOs, as well as academics and other interested parties. On June 25, 1993, the conference adopted the Vienna Declaration and Programme for Action, a document that emphasized the protection of women's, children's, and indigenous people's rights. It also established the office of the High Commissioner for Human Rights (OHCHR), which represented a major organizational step. The process of reform had started.

Agendas and structures in the new millennium

The follow-up to the 1993 Vienna Conference was almost immediate. The first High Commissioner for Human Rights, Ecuadorian judge José Ayala Lasso, took office in April 1994. He was followed by former Irish president Mary Robinson (1997–2002), who had apparently been head-hunted for the job by Secretary-General Kofi Annan. A highly popular and successful politician, Robinson became a tireless global advocate of human rights. The first High Commissioner to visit Chinese-occupied Tibet, Robinson did not shy away from controversial arguments; she even criticized her native Ireland for exploiting foreign workers and attacked the use of capital punishment in the United States.

Upon her retirement in 2002, Robinson was followed by another high-profile High Commissioner, Brazil's Sergio Vieira de Mello. A veteran of a number of refugee crises, de Mello had been a UN "careerist" since the late 1960s. He had won praise in the international press for handling the transition of East Timor (Timor Leste) from Indonesian occupation to independence between 1999 and 2002. Many thought of him as a potential successor to Kofi Annan, but his career ended tragically. In May 2003, de Mello accepted yet another high-profile mission, becoming the Secretary-General's Special Representative to occupied Iraq. In August 2003 de Mello was killed in Baghdad after a terrorist attack. The UN is often criticized for its high-flying and overpaid diplomats. De Mello surely fit that description. Yet the circumstances of his death were a shocking reminder—almost at a par with the death of Secretary-General Dag Hammarskjöld in the Congo during a mediation mission—of the dangers inherent in working for the international organization.

Since de Mello's death, the High Commissioner's office has been occupied by the Canadian human rights lawyer Louise Arbour. Her appointment signaled a shift toward a more legalistic approach. Arbour, a member of Canada's Supreme Court, was the former Chief Prosecutor of War Crimes before the International Criminal Tribunal for Rwanda and the International Criminal Tribunal for the Former Yugoslavia in The Hague. In that capacity she had indicted Yugoslav president Slobodan Milošević for war crimes. The significance of the act was that Milošević was the first serving head of state called to account. Thus, Arbour's term as the High Commissioner was to see the doubling of the efforts at making human rights abusers face trial.

In addition to the sheer force of the personalities that have served in the post, the establishment of the High Commissioner's office was a landmark shift in a number of other ways. Holding the rank of UN Under-Secretary-General, the OHCHR is near the top of the UN's hierarchy. Headquartered in Geneva, the OHCHR has established a global presence by creating a network of regional and country offices and by assigning human rights advisors to individual areas. All of this activity—as well as a general push to emphasize a human rights agenda by successive UN Secretaries-General (Boutros Boutros-Ghali and Kofi Annan)—has had a positive impact. In the twenty-first century it has become increasingly difficult for human rights violations to go unnoticed.

Unfortunately, this does not mean that such violations have ended. In its first few years of operation the OHCHR had to face to a series of crises, such as ethnic cleansing in former Yugoslavia (including the 1995 Srebrenica massacre of Bosniaks by Serbs) and the 1994 genocide in Rwanda that resulted in the systematic killing of an estimated 800,000 ethnic Tutsis. In the end, even the most energetic of High Commissioners, such as Mary Robinson, could do little to stop determined violators from ignoring the basic principles of human rights, be they the Taliban in Afghanistan, Saddam Hussein's regime in Iraq, communist governments in China or—much worse—in North Korea, or the many one-party dictatorships in sub-Saharan Africa.

Such black spots did not mean that there was no progress. In Central America, democratization progressed as the region left behind a long legacy of right-wing totalitarian rule and human rights abuses. To make sure that progress toward implementing good human rights practices is being made, the OHCHR works with national governments and occasionally, as it did in 2004 in Guatemala, opens field offices in order to monitor developments in particular countries. In many parts of Africa, the OHCHR's thirteen field offices exert similar control and pressure—assuring that everything from children's rights to voting rights is being observed. The challenges are great. Since its transformation from apartheid to democracy, South Africa has stood as a hopeful example of the steps taken forward in the advancement of human rights. Yet, in 2007 the OHCHR's South African Bureau in Pretoria listed a staggering number of goals for its operations, ranging from educational campaigns to pressuring the government into improving its efforts to protect minorities and marginalized groups.

In fact, the biggest challenge for the OHCHR is the sheer number of issues—or abuses—that it has to deal with. In one week in November 2007, for example, the OHCHR was holding meetings on arbitrary detention, lobbying to secure the rights of indigenous people in the Amazon rain forest, demanding an end to violence against women in the Middle East and Africa, and having committee discussions on the rights of migrant workers and their families. The ultimate irony though is that no matter what this or that commission or working group in Geneva decided to recommend, the OHCHR had very few tools of implementation.

The International Criminal Court and the Human Rights Council

The paradox between massive abuses and encouraging improvements in the world's human rights record pointed to a need for further strengthening the existing UN structure. In the early twenty-first century this resulted in two important developments.

First, there was the establishment of the International Criminal Court (ICC) in 2002. Headquartered in The Hague, the ICC became a permanent tribunal to prosecute individuals for genocide, crimes against humanity, and war crimes. To be sure, the ICC suffers from several weaknesses: it can prosecute only crimes committed after July 1, 2002; it cannot prosecute individuals for crimes of aggression; and a number of countries have not become members of the ICC.

Most importantly, although President Clinton signed the founding treaty of the ICC (the Rome Statute), in late 2000 (the treaty establishing the ICC was actually negotiated in 1998), he immediately announced that he would not submit it to the Congress for ratification until several changes were made. In 2002, the Bush administration informed the UN that it had no intention of joining the ICC. There was little surprising in this American attitude. Both presidents were, in fact, reflecting a bipartisan consensus in the United States that considered the ICC to be an infringement on American national sovereignty. "It is an agreement that is harmful to the national interests of the United States, and harmful to our presence abroad," commented John Bolton, the Bush administration's ambassador to the UN. Basically, the Democrats and Republicans tended to share a broad agreement over the fact that only American courts should be allowed to judge American citizens. Another argument against the ICC was that since Americans were serving abroad in more than one hundred countries, they could be subjected to "frivolous or politically motivated persecutions."[3] Not for the first time, nationalism collided with universalism at the UN.

Second, the UN Commission on Human Rights (UNCHR) was replaced by the UN Human Rights Council (UNHRC) in 2006. Aside from the name change, the major purpose of the change was to address the criticism often targeted at the commission: that it tended to give high-profile positions to countries that were well-known abusers of human rights. In this regard, the 2003 election of Libya to the chairmanship of UNCHR had been the last straw to the growing body of skeptics. Thus, over the next few years the statutes of the UNHRC were drafted, negotiated, and, on March 15, 2006, voted upon. The resolution calling for the establishment of the UNHRC specifically stated that "members elected to the [Human Rights] Council shall uphold the highest standards in the promotion and protection of human rights." The resolution passed with surprising unanimity: 170 members (out of a total of 191) voted affirmatively at the General Assembly.[4]

Only four countries voted against; among these was, as in the case of the ICC, the United States. Like the Marshall Islands, Palau, and Israel, the Americans claimed that the Human Rights Council would suffer from exactly the same problems as its predecessor: it would have too little power and would easily be overtaken by countries that abused human rights on a regular basis. In fact, a number of such countries, including Belarus, the Central African Republic, Iran, Liberia, North Korea, and Venezuela, abstained from the vote.

The critics were not entirely off the mark: many of the changes were cosmetic. Instead of the fifty-three-member UNCHR, the UNHRC would have forty-seven seats, each representing one of the UN member countries. Such streamlining aside, the seats are distributed among the UN's regional groups as follows: thirteen for Africa, thirteen for Asia, six for Eastern Europe, eight for Latin America and the Caribbean, and seven for Western Europe and Oceania. The countries are elected for three-year terms (renewable once) by a majority vote at the General Assembly, in a secret ballot. As an additional check any council member may be suspended by a two-thirds vote of the General Assembly. This apportionment may seem democratic in terms of the distribution of the globe's population, but it hardly did justice to the fact that it might be difficult—at any given time—to find thirteen countries in Asia or Africa with acceptable (let alone exemplary) human rights records. In 2007, for example, Nigeria, the People's Republic of China, and Azerbaijan were members despite being under criticism for their respective governments' abuse of power.

Perhaps the most glaring controversy regarding the Human Rights Council—as well as the overall human rights regime (including the ICC) in the twenty-first century—is the role of the United States. As a result of its refusal to join the ICC, a number of European countries cooperated in voting the United States out of the Commission on Human Rights in 2001. Although it was allowed to return two years later, the United States responded by boycotting both the ICC and the UNHRC. What has kept the United States out of the new human rights regime is, basically, the same conundrum that has handicapped the UN in so many other fields as well: the contradicting demands of national sovereignty and national security on the one hand, and universalism on the other hand. At the same time the American government continues to portray itself as a champion of human rights; indeed when compared to many members of the UNHRC or the ICC, Washington's record was practically sublime until the outbreak of news regarding the abuse of terrorist suspects at the American base in Guantanamo Bay, Cuba, in 2003, and the use of torture by Americans at the Abu Ghraib prison camp in Iraq in 2004.

It is perhaps understandable that Americans would not want their citizens dragged in front of the ICC for, say, war crimes in Iraq. But by remaining outside the ICC and the UNHRC, the Americans send an unfortunate signal to other governments, which are engaged in large-scale human rights abuses, to follow suit.

The question that faces the UN as a result is how to address the consequences of the inevitable violations of human rights. The ICC, for example, was created to address one part of the challenge: the need to bring to justice those that had committed crimes. But that remains a long-drawn-out process.

Human security and the "responsibility to protect"

The term "human security" became common usage after the 1975 Helsinki Conference on Security and Cooperation in Europe. The signing of the so-called Helsinki Accords in early August 1975 was a remarkable feat of multilateral diplomacy: thirty-five European countries as well as the United States, Canada, and the Soviet Union agreed on a document that established such basic rules as the inviolability of post-1945 borders in Europe. Most controversially at the time, however, the Helsinki Accords included a number of clauses—hidden in "Basket III" of the document—that emphasized respect for human rights as an important element of international security. The 1975 agreements therefore indicated a shift from a narrow state-centered concern over security to a more all-encompassing one. The rights of individuals and human linkages across national borders were given a special place alongside more traditional questions of borders. At the height of the Cold War a motto from the Helsinki conference captured the basic idea: "Security is not gained by erecting fences; security is enhanced by building bridges."

In the twenty-first century "human security" has entered into common usage as shorthand for the concerns and practices that deal with the many faces of, and close relations between, freedom from fear and freedom from want. Reflecting the significance of the concept, Secretary-General Kofi Annan established the Commission on Human Security (CHS) in early 2001. The commission delivered its final report in 2003, proposing:

> a new security framework that centers directly and specifically on people. Human security focuses on shielding people from critical and pervasive threats and empowering them to take charge of their lives. It demands creating genuine opportunities for people to live in safety and dignity and earn their livelihood.

Human security therefore encompasses numerous issues, the foremost of which are the need to fight poverty, improve education, protect children, enhance access to medical care, fight international arms and drugs trade, and protect the environment.

There was no question that all these were serious problems. But there was an irony in all this: the UN already had organizations whose task it was to deal with each of the issues outlined in the CHS's report. The UNDP's fight against poverty was joined by the FAO, the ILO, the International Fund for Agricultural Development (IFAD), and many others. Improving education was the specific goal of UNESCO. Assisting and protecting children was UNICEF's purview. The World Health Organization (WHO) was fighting to improve the access to and quality of medical care. The UN had commissions for fighting arms smuggling and drug trade. The UN Environment Programme (UNEP) does, well, what its name indicates. To a large extent, "human security" was but a new collective noun to explain what the UN was already doing.

Much of this can be summed up by the concept "the Responsibility to Protect," the idea that sovereign states have a responsibility to protect their own citizens from avoidable catastrophe, but that when they are unwilling or unable to do so, that responsibility must be borne by the broader community of states. One group of people whose human security is in constant jeopardy and whose human rights are frequently trampled upon is refugees.

Refugees, displaced persons, and the UNHCR

Since the dawn of time people have fled their homelands and been unable or unwilling to return because they fear persecution. In many cases the cause of a refugee problem has been military conquest; in others it may have been a regime that, once installed in power, has started persecuting a group of people within the nation's borders (for instance, Jews in Nazi Germany). Whatever the cause of a specific refugee question, it is warfare and the movement of national boundaries that has traditionally been the greatest cause of what is generally referred to as forced migration. And it is a phenomenon as old as warfare itself.

Only in the twentieth century, however, did refugee issues attract global attention. After World War I, millions of people were displaced throughout Europe and other regions of conflict. The first international agency dealing with refugee problems, the High Commission for Refugees, was established by the League of Nations in 1921. Its original mission was to deal with approximately 1.5 million refugees fleeing the Russian Revolution and civil war, but the scope was soon extended to cover Armenians, Assyrians, and Turks. In 1931 the High Commission became the Nansen International Office for Refugees (so named after Fridtjof Nansen, head of the High Commission, who had died in 1930).

Funded mainly by private contributions, the Nansen Office, much like its successors, was plagued by inadequate funding and the uncooperative attitude of many countries. Nevertheless, the Nansen Office did record a few important achievements, including the establishment of the so-called Nansen passport, issued by the League of Nations to stateless refugees. They were designed in 1922 and initially given to refugees fleeing the Russian Revolution. Approximately 450,000 Nansen passports, honored by fifty-two countries, were issued between 1922 and 1942. Nansen also prompted the creation of a special office for refugees fleeing persecution in Nazi Germany, and the first international legal instrument to protect the rights of refugees: the Refugee Convention of 1933 (signed by only thirteen nations). It is estimated that the Nansen Office helped approximately a million refugees before it was abolished at the end of 1938.

The number of refugees multiplied during and after World War II. Although already a global issue, the handling of refugees was mostly a European problem at the time. It included the millions who escaped Nazi persecution (including European Jews) and fled invading German (and Italian) armies. When the tide of war turned in the Allies' favor, the Germans themselves constituted a large refugee group. All in all, few areas of Europe were unaffected by the mass movement of civilians. In the Far East, large areas of China saw similar crises resulting from the Japanese advances. Estimates of the number of refugees and internally displaced persons at the end of World War II range from 11 to 20 million.

In 1943 the Allies created the United Nations Relief and Rehabilitation Administration (UNRRA) to deal with this challenge. In subsequent years the UNRRA provided aid to areas liberated from German or Japanese occupation in Europe and Asia. This included returning more than 7 million refugees to their country of origin and setting up displaced persons camps for 1 million refugees who refused to be repatriated. When UNRRA was shut down in 1949, its refugee-related tasks were handed to the International Refugee Organization (IRO). A year later the IRO became the United Nations High Commissioner for Refugees (UNHCR). Its initial mandate was for three years, probably considered sufficient for the resettlement of the remaining 1.2 million European refugees. As it happened, starting in 1953 the mandate was renewed repeatedly every five years. Only in 2003 did the General Assembly remove the time limit and make UNHCR permanent "until the refugee problem is solved."

Categories of "people of concern to UNHCR"

There are millions of people who have become homeless and are in desperate circumstances but do not legally qualify as refugees (and are therefore not eligible for normal relief or protection). Thus, UNHCR activities have been broadened and include at least the following groups:

Refugees (ca. 8.4 million in 2006)

People who have fled their homeland and sought sanctuary in a second country in order to escape persecution, war, terrorism, extreme poverty, famines, and natural disaster.

Internally displaced people (7.1 million)

People who have fled their homes, generally during a civil war, but have stayed in their native countries rather than seeking refuge abroad.

Stateless people (3.3 million)

People without citizenship as a result of several possible circumstances: (a) the state that gave their previous nationality may have ceased to exist and there is no successor state; (b) their nationality has been repudiated by their own state; (c) they are members of a group that is denied citizen status in the country in whose territory they are born, etc.

Returnees (1.1 million)

People who have returned to their own countries but still receive help from UNHCR in their reintegration.

Asylum seekers (770,000)

People who have asked for refugee status but are still awaiting decision.

The problem seems unsolvable. Based on past experience, there is little hope that the refugee question will disappear. Although European World War II refugees were for the most parts either repatriated or resettled by the early 1950s, other crises conspired to keep the size of the globe's refugee populations high (and growing). Since the 1950s the UNHCR has helped an estimated 50 million people to restart their lives. But problems keep multiplying. In 1955 the estimated global refugee population was 2.2 million; by the mid-1960s the number had gone up to 11 million; in 1995 it was 14 million. In 2007 UNHCR's staff of 7,000 was attending to the needs of more than 20 million people in 116 countries. The figure included refugees as well as other "people of concern" to UNHCR: internally displaced persons, people rendered stateless, returnees, and asylum seekers.

Aside from the sheer growth in numbers, the geographical distribution of refugees has changed. In the 1950s more than half of UNHCR's "clientele" were in Europe. But the 1960s and 1970s saw an expanding role for UNHCR in the developing world, particularly in Asia and Africa. In the early 1970s the scope of the humanitarian crisis on the Indian subcontinent—where more than 10 million Bengalis fled the Pakistani Army's repression into India in 1970—exposed UNHCR to many new challenges, including the management of sudden mass refugee influxes, the construction of extensive refugee camps, and the procurement and distribution of food and basic relief supplies on a scale previously unimagined. By the 1980s virtually all of UNHCR's activity was in the developing world as it emerged as a truly global organization. This growth has continued over the past decades, even as UNHCR, given its dependency on voluntary contributions, has suffered from constant funding shortages (its 2007 annual budget was around $1 billion).

UNHCR activities, like almost everything the UN does, raise mixed feelings of admiration and frustration. As recognition for its important work UNHCR has won two Nobel Peace Prizes (1955 and 1981), a distinction exceeded only by the International Committee of the Red Cross. UNHCR has been and, sadly, is likely to remain one of the most significant humanitarian aid organizations in the world. Sadly, because as humanitarian emergencies have increased in scale and complexity, UNHCR's ability to maintain its role as a neutral relief organization has been challenged. At times refugees have been recruited as warriors in civil wars (for instance, Angola since the 1970s or Afghanistan since the 1980s). Humanitarian aid, unfortunately, occasionally ends up being used to fund arms purchases rather than to help refugees. Indeed, refugee camps themselves are not something most governments wish to see on their territory because of their tendency to spread the conflict that caused the refugees to flee in the first place. Prolonged existence in refugee camps, a result of prolonged conflicts often fueled by assistance from the main rivals in the Cold War, only exacerbates these problems.

Nor does an end to such existence naturally solve problems. With the end of the Cold War, many prolonged conflicts came to an end. Millions of refugees were repatriated to countries in Africa and Asia. But a new problem arose: the need to assist returnees who had spent more than a decade away to reintegrate into home communities whose social and economic infrastructure in many cases had been destroyed. For example, two years after the return of 45,000 refugees to Namibia in Southwest Africa, only 75 percent had found employment.

Multiplication of refugee problems

In the twenty-first century UNHCR thus faces a myriad of different challenges. Refugee repatriation threatens to destabilize the countries that want their long-lost brethren back. New refugees continue to appear. The American-led intervention in Afghanistan in 2001 and the invasion and occupation of Iraq in 2003 created

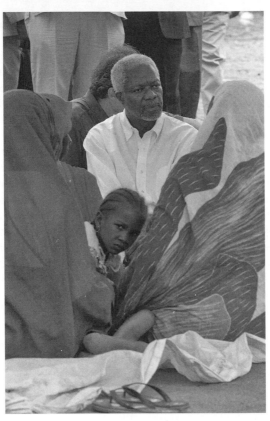

11. Secretary-General Kofi Annan talking to women in the Zam Zam displaced persons camp in the Darfur region of Sudan in 2004.

massive movements of people in and out of these two countries (thus producing challenges both of repatriation and refugees). In 2006–07 debates over whether genocide was under way in the Darfur region of western Sudan masked the depressing fact that the crisis had produced 2.5 million refugees. It is a sad measure of the state of the world that a "temporary" relief organization created more than a half century ago looks set to limp on for decades to come.

Largely as a response to the multiplying challenges of the post–Cold War era, UNHCR issued the Agenda for Protection in 2002. It stressed the need for multilateral cooperation in meeting the international community's responsibility to protect individuals who were in harm's way due to circumstances outside their control. Logically, the document stressed the need to share burdens and responsibilities and search for durable (security-related) solutions. It also outlined one area in need of specific attention: the needs of refugee women and children.

None of this was entirely new or groundbreaking. UNHCR had, in fact, a long-standing cooperation with numerous UN and other agencies dealing with human security issues. These included the World Food Program (WFP), UNICEF, the World Health Organization (WHO), UNDP, OHCHR, the International Committee of the Red Cross (ICRC), the World Bank, and the International Organization for Migration (IOM). Almost six hundred nongovernmental organizations have worked with UNHCR. Such cooperation has been essential for effective refugee aid. Over the past six decades, notwithstanding some of the faults in the refugee protection and assistance system, it remains an indispensable and, on the whole, successful part of the effort to protect the globe's most vulnerable groups of people.

The enduring paradox of human rights

There is no getting around the paradox. On the one hand, human rights have been a central part of the UN's agenda from the very beginning, and there has been success in raising the levels of respect for many of the individual rights as defined in the 1948 Universal Declaration. On the other hand, the global respect for human rights has remained contingent on the vagaries of the international environment and the whims of nation-states. Human rights, even as they are undoubtedly more diligently monitored in the twenty-first century than ever before, are constantly violated on every continent.

The same sad truth applies to those whose human rights are most easily trampled upon: refugees. Lacking the protection of the state, the lives of millions of people "of concern" to the UNHCR ultimately depend on the goodwill of the international community, but the protection of their human rights easily clashes with the rights of a nation-state (whether the one the refugees have escaped from or are temporarily settled in).

In other words, the estimated 4 million internally displaced people in Sudan are rightly a concern to UNHCR, but they may also represent a potential threat to the Sudanese government's hold on power (notwithstanding any moral issues involved) and thus a danger to the survival of the nation-state. Similarly, the arrival in neighboring Chad of hundreds of thousands of refugees from Sudan's Darfur region since 2003 represents a humanitarian emergency of massive proportions that demands large-scale international action. But the organization of twelve large refugee camps also presents a potential threat to the nascent democracy of the host nation, Chad. Starting in 2005 this became painfully clear as the Darfur conflict spread to Chad's eastern parts. In addition, Chad suddenly had to address another problem: by 2007 there were an estimated 150,000 internally displaced Chadians competing for the attentions of UNHCR with 220,000 Sudanese refugees.

The Darfur crisis is but one example of three salient facts about human rights and the United Nations. First, respect for human rights remains fragile in many parts of the globe. Second, no universal declaration, investigative commission, special rapporteur, or international organization can act as a magic fix, because ultimately it is those with political authority who define the balance between rights and responsibilities within their territory. Third, hopeless though it may sometimes seem, the UN is particularly indispensable in this area as the only universally recognized body that can, via its many tools, exert pressure on nations to modify their human rights policies and assist those who suffer from the abuse of power still too rampant around the world today.

Chapter 7

Reform and challenges: the future of the United Nations

"If the United Nations is to survive, those who represent it must bolster it; those who advocate it must submit to it; and those who believe in it must fight for it."[1] Norman Cousins, a prominent journalist and peace advocate, uttered these words in 1956. They continue to resonate today, for the UN is hardly a perfect institution. It is structurally flawed and operationally cumbersome. It often lacks the means of implementation even as it may serve as the source of excellent ideas. Its different programs often duplicate work that might be better done by one centralized agency. In short, the UN is in need of reform and support if it is to have a meaningful future.

These issues—reforming the system and obtaining wide international support—are neither new nor separate. Ever since the early 1990s, there has been talk about the need to reform the UN Security Council in order to make it more democratic and representative. Nor was it an accident that the last decade of the twentieth century saw a massive litany of initiatives—or "agendas"—that addressed the key functions of the UN system: peace, democracy (and human rights), and development. In the twenty-first century hardly a day has gone by without complaints and arguments over the way development aid is administered, human rights are not effectively promoted, peace operations are not producing sustained results, and a few countries, most notably the United States, are treating the UN as a mere tool of their policy that can be used, abused, or ignored as those in power in Washington see fit.

And yet, very few would seriously suggest scrapping the UN altogether. It remains indispensable but in need of reform. But how can this impossible hybrid that represents the widely different interests of virtually all inhabitants of this globe be improved? What can be done to enhance the UN's effectiveness in safeguarding international security and helping war-torn societies get back on their feet? In what way could the UN's development policies be changed to improve the chances of success in the long struggle against poverty and all its undesirable side effects? How can the UN safeguard both human security and human rights in a more assertive manner?

Need for reform: the Security Council

How could the Security Council be made more effective as an instrument of solving international disputes? How could it be made more representative of the global community? The question of reforming the UNSC tends to focus on two intertwined issues: veto and membership.

Proposals abound. In the early 1990s a number of countries floated around the idea of abandoning the veto and doubling the size of the Security Council membership. In this way, countries like Germany, Japan, India, and Brazil (all strong candidates for membership) argued, UNSC would become more reflective of the changed global constellation of power.

Two obvious problems, still hindering any serious reform a decade and a half later, became evident. First, any attempt to remove the veto was bound to be vetoed. There is no provision within the UN Charter that would allow the removal of the veto right without the P-5's unanimous consent. But why would China, France, Great

Britain, Russia, or the United States give up this obvious trump card? Moreover, the veto had been conceived in order to keep the five countries, especially the United States, in the organization by enabling them to block decisions they would have found against their national interests.

Second, the addition of new permanent members—with or without the right of veto—has run into many objections from countries that either feel they should be in serious contention for such a privileged position and/or have a strained relationship with a potential candidate country. Many Europeans, for example, object to Germany's membership; Argentina sees little merit in having Brazil elevated to new heights; and Pakistan looks at India's council bid with distinct animosity.

This, basically, means that the Security Council is destined to remain undemocratic and virtually unchanged. While its composition may be tinkered with, there is not going to be a dramatic overhaul; an addition of a few new members is possible, but is the creation of permanent seats for certain countries (such as those just mentioned) possible? The P-5 will not give up their powers voluntarily.

Yet, one should not despair. Reforming the veto power of permanent Security Council members—or adding new members to the UNSC—is a much debated and potentially important possibility. But how necessary is it? It alone provides no miracle cure. UNSC resolutions are almost always a compromise, vetoes have been used fairly sparingly over the past six decades, in part because the need to veto is negotiated away, or a mere threat of a veto may lead to the proposal being withdrawn.

In the end, reforming how the UNSC works is hardly the only way of improving the UN's overall effectiveness. In fact, it addresses only a small part of the issues plaguing the organization at the moment and hardly touches upon the "real" issues of the day. For

High-Level panel on threats, challenges, and change

In September 2003, noting that "the events of the past year have exposed deep divisions among members of the United Nations on fundamental questions of policy and principle," UN Secretary-General Kofi Annan created the panel to ensure that the United Nations remains capable of fulfilling its primary purpose as enshrined in article 1 of the charter—"to take effective collective measures for the prevention and removal of threats to the peace."

The panel, consisting of former high-level government officials from around the globe, delivered its report in 2004. It identified six clusters of global threats:

- war between States
- violence within States, including civil wars, large-scale human rights abuses and genocide
- poverty, infectious disease, and environmental degradation
- nuclear, radiological, chemical and biological weapons
- terrorism
- transnational organized crime.

The panel highlighted the fact that the UN was in a position to deal with all such threats, but that it needs to:

Revitalize the **General Assembly** and the **Economic and Social Council**

Restore credibility to the **Commission on Human Rights**

Strengthen the role of the Secretary General in questions of peace and security

Increase the credibility and effectiveness of the **Security Council**—the panel emphasized the need for "making its composition better reflect today's realities"

Create a **Peacebuilding Commission**

Some of these suggestions have since been carried out, most notably the creation of the Peacebuilding Commission in 2006.

the international security challenges faced by the UN today are vastly different than those in earlier decades. As reflected in the Secretary-General's High Panel Report on Global Security Challenges, the world of the twenty-first century is confronted by such concerns as nuclear terrorism, state collapse, and the rapid spread of infectious disease. Viewed in this context, debates over the size of the Security Council and the ins and outs of the veto right are hardly the most pressing issues in the field of international security.

Need for reform: peace operations

The drive toward reforming the UN's peace operations gathered force in the 1990s. A number of questions have been repeatedly raised. How to make most of a limited number of troops in difficult situations? How to prevent abuses of power—in the form of sexual exploitation and human trafficking—by the peacekeepers themselves? How to make sure that a peace operation does not interfere in a country's democratic process and thus create new problems? How to do all this while preventing a repeat of the tragic events in Bosnia, Rwanda, and Somalia in the 1990s?

These and other questions were addressed in the 2000 Brahimi Report on Peacekeeping. The report, not unexpectedly, pointed out the obvious lack of resources that hampered many UN peace operations, emphasized the need for clear and realistic mandates, and heralded the insufficient general strategic planning of operations. But it also, and perhaps most significantly, flagged the need to develop "a rapid deployment capacity" for UN peacekeepers. The report itself provided the backdrop for the creation of the UN Peacebuilding Commission in 2006.

Despite the establishment of this commission, progress and reform along the lines of the Brahimi Report remains limited almost a decade after its initial delivery. To be sure, there are more peacekeepers in more places funded by slightly more money. But

UN peace operations rarely benefit from an integrated support network. Equally important, they lack resources and depend, most of the time, on the ability of the Secretary-General to raise money for a specific operation.

Moreover, as the case of Darfur has yet again shown, the UN cannot simply impose a peacekeeping force on an unwilling host government. Instead, in order to compensate for the lack of political muscle and manpower, the UN has been forced to "outsource" some of its peacekeeping to such regional organizations as the African Union (which represented the bulk of peacekeepers stationed in Sudan in 2007). The results, as far as Darfur can stand as a case study, are hardly comforting: between 2003 and 2007 an estimated 400,000 people were killed while at least 2 million refugees fled Darfur. Talk of genocide and comparisons to Rwanda in 1993–94 were rampant.

Whether such tragedies as Darfur could have been avoided with a more intrusive and aggressive UN policy is difficult to ascertain. In the end, without the support of its member states, and particularly the P-5 of the Security Council, no operational capability would have been meaningful. Nor does the Darfur experience of outsourcing peacekeeping to regional organizations mean that such a practice cannot be successful; NATO's role in Bosnia seems to provide the exact opposite lesson.

In the end, when contemplating the lessons of past peacekeeping and how to make future operations more effective, one comes back to a key point in the Brahimi Report: the need for a rapid deployment capacity. How else but with an ability to send peacekeepers to different corners of the globe at short notice can the UN respond to a sudden crisis? Without such capacity it will always be rendered a second-class outfit called upon to police difficult situations or clean up the mess left by "serious" fighting.

12. Jean-Marie Guéhenno, Under-Secretary-General for Peacekeeping Operations, and Juan Gabriel Valdés, special representative of the Secretary-General and head of the United Nations Stabilization Mission in Haiti, accompany a Brazilian patrol in Bel-Air, a hillside slum in Port-au-Prince ravaged by armed bandits in 2005.

This brings one back to article 45 of the original UN Charter that envisioned a permanent UN air force—provided by the P-5 and based around the globe—held at the discretionary use of the Security Council and commandeered by the Military Staff Committee (that consisted of representatives of the P-5). Something similar—in the form of a permanent and easily deployable UN peacekeeping force—to that never-implemented provision is probably needed for the UN peace operations to emerge as truly effective instruments of international security.

Depending on one's perspective, such a plan might seem either utopian or dangerous. But it may also be necessary.

Need for reform: development

The eight Millennium Development Goals (MDGs) of 2000 constituted the first common global agenda for human development. It was much overdue and received, by and large, an enthusiastic welcome. This is hardly a surprise, for who could seriously challenge the desirability of fighting global poverty?

But there are two basic obstacles. First, the twentieth-century debate over the proper role of market forces seems to have been decisively won by those heralding the importance of free markets. Many argue—and often with convincing evidence—that development aid actually hurts those on the receiving end by creating a dependency from the donors. Whether this is entirely true is difficult to prove. Despite decades of development, masses of people continue to live in abject poverty, and this fact continues to undermine even the most sophisticated argument in favor of sustained development assistance as the best means of bringing about global social and economic justice. It is no wonder that skepticism, well founded or not, abounds.

Second, the manner in which aid is delivered raises the indispensable need for reform. Perhaps because of the complexity of the problem, the effort to combat it has become increasingly fragmented, with the World Bank and the UNDP representing only two of the many organizations involved in administering development assistance. With numerous divisions and agencies working on all aspects of development, the UN has not always effectively marshaled the full strength of its resources. In other words: duplication and overlap have reduced efficiency and increased administrative costs within the UN and its sister organizations.

This is hardly a new problem. In 1997 Secretary-General Kofi Annan had already created the UN Development Group, a body coordinating the work of the major UN agencies, funds, and departments that deal with development issues. The UNDG has encouraged the harmonization of UN development activities nationally and globally. In the past decade further efforts have proliferated, building on the recommendations from the

Millennium Declaration, the 2005 World Summit to assess progress on the MDGs and other development goals, various resolutions of the UN General Assembly, the OECD 2005 Paris Declaration on Aid Effectiveness, and, most recently, the November 2006 recommendations of the High-Level Panel on UN System-Wide Coherence titled *Delivering as One.*

This last report in particular had the potential of making a difference in the overall work of the UN and its development work. The fifteen members of the panel included several presidents and prime ministers, as well as Gordon Brown, who would move to become British Prime Minister in 2007. *Delivering as One* identified UN development assistance as "fragmented and weak." Thus, it called for a well-governed, well-funded UN equipped to meet the changing needs of countries. The report emphasized nation-level planning and execution of development aid. It therefore proposed consolidating most UN country activities under one strategic program, one budgetary framework, one strong country team leader, and one office. In short, it called for centralization at the country level.

This was all reasonable. One of the UN's overall problems is the proliferation of the many agencies that, at least through the eyes of a detached observer, seem to engage in very similar work and competing for often scarce resources. Whether *Delivering as One* will lead to an overhaul of the way UN delivers its development aid, however, remains uncertain. By late 2007 only eight countries had agreed to pilot unified UN activities: Albania, Cape Verde, Mozambique, Pakistan, Rwanda, Tanzania, Uruguay, and Vietnam. Of these only Vietnam has taken serious steps toward implementation.

Given the significance that most analysts of the UN attribute to development aid as an engine of combating poverty and its political side effects, *Delivering as One* clearly addresses a fundamental need for reform within the UN. The significance of

Delivering as One

In 2005 UN Secretary-General Kofi Annan created a High-Level Panel to Study System-Wide Coherence. The essential purpose of the panel was to "explore how the United Nations system could work more coherently and effectively across the world in the areas of development, humanitarian assistance and the environment."

The report of the panel was delivered in November 2006. It made its case for reform as follows: **"The world needs a coherent and strong multilateral framework with the United Nations at its centre to meet the challenges of development, humanitarian assistance, and the environment in a globalising world. The UN needs to overcome its current fragmentation and to deliver as one ... It should enable and support countries to lead their development processes and help address global challenges such as poverty, environmental degradation, disease and conflict."**

The concept of "Oneness" was central to the panel's report that identified a set of five general recommendations for the future:

- Coherence and consolidation of UN activities, in line with the principle of country ownership, at all levels (country, regional, headquarters)

- Establishment of appropriate governance, managerial, and funding mechanisms to empower and support consolidation, and link the performance and results of UN organizations to funding

- Overhaul of business practices of the UN system to ensure focus on outcomes, responsiveness to needs and delivery of results by the UN system, measured against the Millennium Development Goals

- Ensure significant further opportunities for consolidation and effective delivery of One UN through an in-depth review

- Implementation should be undertaken with urgency, but not ill planned and hasty in a manner that could compromise permanent and effective change.

this mission was aptly summed up by Secretary-General Kofi Annan upon his receipt of the Nobel Peace Prize in 2003:

> Beneath the surface of States and nations, ideas and language, lies the fate of individual human beings in need. Answering their needs will be the mission of the United Nations in the century to come.

Among such needs—and hence central to the UN's future mission—is another area in need of reform: the checkered history of humanity's respect for human rights.

Need for reform: human rights

Talk about difficult issues. Like everything on the UN's agenda the struggle to advance human rights has been an uphill one. And yet, as the UN website itself proudly proclaims:

> One of the great achievements of the United Nations is the creation of a comprehensive body of human rights law, which, for the first time in history, provides us with a universal and internationally protected code of human rights, one to which all nations can subscribe and to which all people can aspire.

Indeed. Who could doubt the desirability of having a set of broadly approved texts that "lay down the law" on human rights. The problem is how it can be implemented.

The promise of human rights remains unfulfilled as daily evidence—torture, denial of basic political rights, abject poverty of people—clearly indicates. Over the past decades human rights watch groups have proliferated. But their reports remain gloomy; more awareness has not resulted in obvious practical progress.

The problem in this field is not lack of appropriate bodies. If anything, there are too many of them: the Human Rights Council, the Commission on Human Rights, the Human Rights Committee, the Committee on Economic, Social and Cultural Rights, and the Committee Against Torture are just a few examples. One should also add that human rights concerns are not the exclusive province of these specifically created bodies; almost every part of the UN system addresses, in one fashion or another, questions and problems related to the abuse of human rights.

The problem goes to the very heart of the UN as an organization founded at a specific historical moment when the nation-state still reigned supreme. Many of the compromises that were evident in the UN Charter reflected this inherent tension between universalism and national prerogatives, the Security Council being perhaps the best known example. In today's globalized world that tension has hardly disappeared; if anything, it has been exacerbated. What it translates to in the field of human rights is a basic dilemma: the UN may have created a detailed body of international human rights legislation. Along the way it has produced bodies that can observe and authoritatively report whether these norms are being adhered to in country x or region y. But it has left the implementation of these norms—the follow-up procedures in case of wrongdoing—largely to the nation-states.

The need for reform that is evident with regards to human rights is, in other words, simultaneously simple and difficult to achieve. What is needed is an ability by a recognized body—like the International Criminal Court (ICC) founded in 2002—to stand above the specific interests of nation-states. So far this has been possible only in rare cases when a leader, such as in the prosecution of Liberia's former president Charles Taylor, has lost both his domestic power base and his international patrons. But to imagine nationals of large countries—most obviously those from the P-5— to ever stand trial at The Hague is difficult.

In sum, for the time being human rights violators are likely to be pursued selectively. Universality may be the norm, but it is unlikely to become the practice. No amount of UN reform is likely to fix that.

Final remark

With all its achievements and shortcomings, the UN remains an indispensable part of the global community of the early twenty-first century. If it suddenly disappeared—that is, if its constituent parts were allowed to disintegrate—millions of people around the world would soon be worse off. That, alone, is sufficient cause for upholding and supporting the UN. Yet, in gauging the significance of the United Nations and the possibilities for improving it a few salient points should be kept in mind.

First, the UN cannot be the "*definite* guaranty of peace" that Woodrow Wilson had hoped the League of Nations would be. As long as the concept of nation-state is the basic form of organizing the different entities we know as countries, as long as there is something called the national interest, as long as governments are responsible for the well-being (or lack thereof) of their citizens, the UN will lack the means of acting independently. It remains, in other words, a *tool* of nations, albeit in a world where the threats to security tend to emanate not from nations but rather from either within them or from various transnational groups.

Second, in its more than sixty years of existence, the UN has developed structures and bureaucracies that in some ways are its own worst enemy. For like any organization, the UN is a place where individuals build careers, compete with each other, establish entrenched positions, and resist change. All this makes the UN too easily a target of condemnation. But more importantly, the UN has a tendency not to reform but to build new structures on top of already existing ones. As a result, meager resources often are squandered due to lack of operational coherence. It is a long way off for the UN being able to deliver as one, a challenge that the current UN Secretary-General, Ban Ki-moon, and his staff will have to address.

Third, the UN cannot continue to have a positive impact without a sufficient support base. This lays a primary responsibility for funding the organization to the wealthier countries of the globe. The paradox is evident: it translates to the wealthy few paying for operations and policies that are mainly directed toward helping others. One of the greatest future challenges will be for the richest member states—particularly, but not exclusively, the United States and the countries of the European Union—to explain to their citizens why a proportion, however small, of their national income should be used to fund the numerous UN operations. Meeting this challenge successfully will determine, if not the future existence of the UN, then at least the effectiveness of the organization.

In the end, the UN cannot and should not be expected to offer solutions to all of the world's ills. It does much good humanitarian work and often provides ways of easing tension and solving crises. It often enables people stuck in poverty to improve their lot. The UN is hardly perfect. But it remains an indispensable organization even as its behavior and effectiveness—much like that of individual countries—is in constant need of improvement.

Chronology

1865	The International Telecommunication Union (ITU) founded.
1874	The Universal Postal Union founded.
1899	The International Peace Conference, held in The Hague, establishes the Permanent Court of Arbitration.
1919	The League of Nations founded. Woodrow Wilson receives the Nobel Peace Prize for his role in the founding of the League of Nations.
1921	First High Commission for Refugees established.
1922	The Permanent Court of International Justice (PCIJ) created.
1931	The Nansen International Office for Refugees established.
1933	High Commission for Refugees Coming from Germany established. Refugee Convention signed by thirteen countries.
1938	The Nansen Office receives the Nobel Peace Prize but is abolished and replaced by the Office of the High Commissioner for Refugees under the Protection of the League.
1942	January 1, the first Declaration of the United Nations by twenty-six countries fighting against the Axis in World War II.
1943	United Nations Relief and Rehabilitation Administration (UNRRA) established.
1944	Dumbarton Oaks conference (China, the UK, the U.S., and the USSR) sets down the general aims and structure of the future UN.

1945	At the Yalta conference in February Churchill, Roosevelt and Stalin affirm their resolve to form a universal organization. In June in San Francisco fifty nations approve the Charter of the United Nations. Former U.S. Secretary of State Cordell Hull awarded the Nobel Peace Prize for his role in the founding of the UN.
1946	First General Assembly and Security Council Session held in London. International Court of Justice (ICJ) replaces PCIJ. Trygve Lie (Norway) becomes the first UN Secretary-General. UN Commission on Human Rights (UNCHR) established.
1948	Universal Declaration of Human Rights. First UN observer mission established—the UN Truce Supervision Organization (UNTSO) in Palestine.
1949	The UN Military Observer Group in India and Pakistan (UNMOGIP) dispatched to oversee the situation in the disputed Kashmir region.
1950	Korean War begins. UN High Commissioner for Refugees (UNHCR) established.
1952	Trygve Lie resigns as UNSG.
1953	Dag Hammarskjöld (Sweden) becomes UNSG.
1954	UNHCR receives the Nobel Peace Prize.
1955	Fifteen countries join the United Nations.
1956	The UN Emergency Force (UNEF), the first UN peacekeeping force, sent to the Suez Canal.
1957	Lester Pearson receives the Nobel Peace Prize for his role in creating the UNEF.
1960	Seventeen newly independent states, sixteen from Africa, join the UN, the biggest increase in membership in any one year. UN Operation in the Congo (ONUC) established to oversee the transition from Belgian rule to independence; transformed into the first peace enforcement operation (mandate ends in 1964).

1961	Hammarskjöld killed, replaced by U Thant (Burma/Myanmar) as UNSG
	Hammarskjöld awarded the Nobel Peace Prize posthumously.
1962	UN membership is more than one hundred.
1964	UN peacekeepers sent to Cyprus.
1965	United Nations Development Programme (UNDP) founded.
	UNICEF awarded the Nobel Peace Prize.
1966	General Assembly strips South Africa of its mandate to govern South-West Africa (Namibia).
	Mandatory sanctions are imposed against Rhodesia (now Zimbabwe) by the Security Council.
	General Assembly adopts the International Covenant on Civil and Political Rights, and the International Covenant on Economic, Social and Cultural Rights. Together with the 1948 Universal Declaration these form the International Bill of Rights.
1967	Egypt asks UNEF to leave; soon afterwards the Six-Day War breaks out, followed by the Security Council adoption of Resolution 242 as the basis for achieving peace in the Middle East.
1968	General Assembly approves the Treaty on the Non-Proliferation of Nuclear Weapons.
1969	ILO awarded the Nobel Peace Prize.
1971	People's Republic of China takes the seat of the Republic of China (Taiwan) at the UN Security Council.
1972	Kurt Waldheim (Austria) becomes UNSG.
	First UN Environment Conference is held in Stockholm, Sweden, leading to the establishment of the UN Environment Programme (UNEP), headquartered in Nairobi.
1974	General Assembly grants the Palestinian Liberation Organization (PLO) observer status.
1975	International Women's Year, highlighted by the first UN conference on women in Mexico City.

1978	General Assembly convenes, for the first time, a conference on disarmament. UN membership is more than 150.
1980	World Health Organization (WHO) officially declares smallpox eradicated.
1981	UN High Commissioner for Refugees is awarded the Nobel Peace Prize.
1982	Javier Pérez de Cuéllar (Peru) becomes UNSG.
1988	UN Peacekeeping operations awarded the Nobel Peace Prize.
1990	UNICEF convenes the World Summit for Children.
1991	Boutros Boutros-Ghali (Egypt) becomes UNSG. After sixteen years of civil war in Angola, a peace agreement negotiated under UN auspices is signed in New York.
1992	The Earth Summit in Rio de Janeiro leads to Agenda 21, a comprehensive plan to promote sustainable development. The UNSG issues "An Agenda for Peace" (highlighting the significance of preventive diplomacy, peacemaking, peacekeeping, and peacebuilding).
1994	UNSG issues "An Agenda for Development."
1995	The World Summit for Social Development meets in Copenhagen, Denmark, to renew the commitment to combating poverty, unemployment, and social exclusion.
1996	The General Assembly adopts the Comprehensive Nuclear Test-Ban Treaty. UNSG issues the Agenda for Democratization.
1997	Kofi Annan (Ghana) becomes UNSG.
2000	General Assembly adopts the Millennium Development Goals The Brahimi Report on UN Peace Operations.
2001	United Nations and Secretary-General Kofi Annan awarded the Nobel Peace Prize.
2002	International Criminal Court (ICC) is established.
2004	A report titled "A More Secure World" by the High Level Panel on Threats, Challenges, and Change calls for global measures to combat environmental threats, terrorism, and other transnational problems.

2005	The International Atomic Energy Agency and its head Mohammed ElBaradei receive the Nobel Peace Prize.
2006	General Assembly resolution (April) establishes the Human Rights Council. Montenegro joins the UN as the 192nd member state. UN Peacebuilding Commission is established. "Delivering as One" report by a High Level Panel outlines the need to reform UN development aid operations.
2007	Ban Ki-moon (South Korea) becomes UNSG. In March, citing Teheran's refusal to end its development of a nuclear weapons capability, the UN Security Council unanimously strengthens economic sanctions against Iran. In May, the UN launches "The International Compact with Iraq" to help establish economic and human security in the war-torn nation. A joint UN-African Union peacekeeping force (UNAMID) enters Sudan's Darfur region.
2008	In March, the UN Security Council further extends economic and travel sanctions against Iran as the Iranian government continues its nuclear program. In May, the ruling military junta in Myanmar allows UN humanitarian aid workers into the country after a disastrous cyclone hit the nation. After earthquakes in Sizhuan province numerous UN organizations participate for the first time in large-scale humanitarian operations in the People's Republic of China. In June, the World Food Summit in Rome, addresses the prospect of rapidly rising global food prices. More than four billion dollars of additional aid to fight hunger and improve agricultural development in the worst affected regions are pledged.

Glossary: acronyms of major UN organs and agencies used in the text

ECOSOC	Economic and Social Council
FAO	Food and Agricultural Organization
GATT	General Agreement on Tariffs and Trade
IAEA	International Atomic Energy Agency
ICJ	International Court of Justice
ILO	International Labor Organization
IMF	International Monetary Fund
ITU	International Telegraph Union
MSC	Military Staff Committee
OHCHR	Office of the High Commissioner for Human Rights
ONUC	United Nations Operation in the Congo
UNCHR	United Nations Commission on Human Rights
UNCTAD	United Nations Conference on Trade and Development
UNDP	United Nations Development Programme
UNEP	United Nations Environment Programme
UNESCO	United Nations Education
UNFPA	United Nations Population Fund
UNGA	United Nations General Assembly
UNHCR	United Nations High Commissioner for Refugees
UNHRC	United Nations Human Rights Council
UNICEF	United Nations Children's Fund

UNMOGIP	UN Military Observer Group in India and Pakistan
UNSC	United Nations Security Council
UNSG	United Nations Secretary General
UNTSO	United Nations Truce Supervision Organization
WFP	World Food Program
WHO	World Health Organization
WTO	World Trade Organization

Glossary

References

Introduction

1. Henry Cabot Lodge, cited in James B. Simpson, *Simpson's Contemporary Quotations* (New York: Houghton Mifflin, 1988).

Chapter 1

1. Woodrow Wilson, quoted from *Congressional Record*, 65th Cong., 3rd sess., Senate Document No. 389, 12–15.
2. Kofi Annan, "Nobel Peace Prize Acceptance speech," December 10, 2001, Oslo, Norway. http://nobelpeaceprize.org/eng_lect_2001b.html

Chapter 2

1. Hammarskjöld interview in *Time* magazine, June 27, 1955.
2. Trygve Lie, cited in James Barros, *Trygve Lie and the Cold War: The UN Secretary General Pursues Peace* (De Kalb, IL: Northern Illinois University Press, 1989), 341.

Chapter 3

1. Bhutto, cited in *New York Times*, Dec. 16, 1971.

Chapter 4

1. Pearson Speech in Irwin Abrams, *Words of Peace: The Nobel Peace Prize Laureates of the Twentieth Century—Selections from Their Acceptance Speeches* (New York: Newmarket Press, 2003).
2. As explained on the UN's website: www.un.org/peace/ peacebuilding/
3. Ibid.

Chapter 5

1. Albornoz, cited in the *New York Times*, Sept. 22, 1985.
2. *Concept and Measurement of Human Development. Human Development Report, 1990*, can be found on: http://hdr.undp.org/ en/reports.
3. *Development and International Economic Cooperation: An Agenda for Development*, can be found at: www.un.org/Docs/SG/ ag_index.htm.
4. *Globalization with a Human Face: 1999 Human Development Report*, can be found on: http://hdr.undp.org/en/reports/global/ hdr1999/

Chapter 6

1. Dag Hammarskjöld's speech at the 180th anniversary of Virginia Declaration of Human Rights, May 20, 1956, cited in Peter B. Heller, *The United Nations under Dag Hammarskjöld, 1953–1961* (Lanham, MD: Scarecrow Press, 2001), 147.
2. Roosevelt, cited in http://www.udhr.org/history/Biographies/ Iiloir l ltiiiii
3. John Bolton's remarks to the Federalist Society, Nov. 14, 2002, can be found on the State Department website: www.state.gov/ t/us/rm/15158.htm.
4. UN General Assembly Resolution 60/251, www.ohchr.org/ english/bodies/hrcouncil/docs/A.RES.60.251_En.pdf

Chapter 7

1. *Saturday Review*, Apr. 15, 1980.

Further reading

It goes without saying that the literature on the various aspects of the UN is vast and the suggestions provided here necessarily limited. Some of the best general accounts covering most aspects of the world organization include: Frederick H. Gareau, *The United Nations and Other International Institutions: A Critical Analysis* (Chicago: Burnham, 2002); Thomas G. Weiss, David P. Forsythe, and Roger A. Coate, *The United Nations and Changing World Politics* (Boulder, CO: Westview, 2004). One can also benefit from reviewing the UN's own *Basic Facts about the United Nations* (New York: United Nations, 2004, or later edition) and Thomas G. Weiss and Sam Daws, *The Oxford Handbook on the United Nations* (New York: Oxford University Press, 2007). For a readable general history and evaluations of the UN readers can turn to Paul Kennedy, *The Parliament of Man: The Past, Present and Future of the United Nations* (New York: Random House, 2007).

Chapter 1: The best hope of mankind? A brief history of the UN

Burgess, Stephen F. *The United Nations under Boutros Boutros-Ghali, 1992–1997*. Lanham, MD: Scarecrow Press, 2001.

Firestone, Bernard J. *The United Nations under U Thant, 1961–1971*. Lanham, MD: Scarecrow Press, 2001.

Gaglione, Anthony. *The United Nations under Trygve Lie, 1945–1953*. Lanham, MD: Scarecrow Press, 2001.

Heller, Peter B. *The United Nations under Dag Hammarskjöld, 1953–1961*. Lanham, MD: Scarecrow Press, 2001.

Lankevich, George J. The *United Nations under Javier Pérez de Cuéllar, 1982–1991*. Lanham, MD: Scarecrow Press, 2001.

Mingst, Karen, and Margaret Karns. *The United Nations in the 21st Century (Dilemmas in World Politics)*. Boulder, CO: Westview, 2006.

Ryan, James Daniel. *The United Nations under Kurt Waldheim, 1972–1981*. Lanham, MD: Scarecrow Press, 2001.

Schlesinger, Stephen. *Act of Creation: The Founding of the United Nations: A Story of Superpowers, Secret Agents, Wartime Allies and Enemies, and Their Quest for a Peaceful World*. Boulder, CO: Westview, 2003.

Traub, James. *Best of Intentions: Kofi Annan and the UN in the Era of American Power*. New York: Farrar, Straus and Giroux, 2006.

Chapter 2: An impossible hybrid: the structure of the UN

Alger, Chadwick. *The United Nations System*. Santa Barbara, CA: ABC-CLIO, 2006.

Fasulo, Linda. *An Insider's Guide to the UN*. New Haven, CT: Yale University Press, 2003.

Gordenker, Leon. *The UN Secretary-General and Secretariat*. London: Routledge, 2005.

Jolly, Richard. *The UN and Bretton Woods Institutions*. New York: St. Martin's, 1995.

Peterson, M.J. *The United Nations General Assembly*. London: Routledge, 2005.

Taylor, Paul, and A. J. R. Groom, eds. *The United Nations at the Millennium: The Principal Organs*. London and New York: Continuum, 2000.

Chapter 3: Facing wars, confronting threats: the UN Security Council in action

Gharekhan, Chinmaya. *The Horseshoe Table: An Inside View of the UN Security Council*. New York: Longman, 2006.

Krasno, Jean E., and James S. Sutterlin. *The United Nations and Iraq: Defanging the Viper*. Westport, CT: Praeger, 2003.

Luck, Edward C. *The UN Security Council: A Primer*. London: Routledge, 2006.

Malone, David. *The UN Security Council: From the Cold War to the 21st Century*. Boulder, CO: Lynne Rienner, 2004.

Pugh, Michael, and Waheguru Pal Singh Sidhu, eds., *The United Nations & Regional Security: Europe and Beyond*. Boulder, CO: Lynne Rienner, 2003.

Sutterlin, James S. *The United Nations and the Maintenance of International Security: A Challenge to Be Met*. Westport, CT: Praeger, 2003.

Chapter 4: Peacekeeping to peacebuilding

Boulden, Jane. *The United Nations and Mandate Enforcement: Congo, Somalia, and Bosnia*. Kingston, Ontario: Centre for International Relations, Queen's University, 1999.

Doyle, Michael. *Making War and Building Peace: United Nations Peace Operations*. Princeton: Princeton University Press, 2006.

Hill, Stephen. *United Nations Disarmament Processes in Intra-state Conflict*. New York: Palgrave Macmillan, 2004.

LeBor, Adam. *"Complicity with Evil": The United Nations in an Age of Modern Genocide*. New Haven, CT: Yale University Press, 2006.

Paris, Roland. *At War's End: Building Peace After Civil Conflict*. New York: Cambridge University Press, 2004.

Russett, Bruce, and John O'Neal, *Triangulating Peace: Democracy, Interdependence, and International Organizations*. New York: Norton, 2001.

Thakur, Ramesh. *The United Nations, Peace and Security: From Collective Security to the Responsibility to Protect*. New York: Cambridge University Press, 2006.

Chapter 5: Economic development to human development

Berthelot, Yves, ed. *Unity and Diversity in Development Ideas: Perspectives from the UN Regional Commissions*. Bloomington: Indiana University Press, 2004.

Emmerij, Louis, Richard Jolly, and Thomas G. Weiss. *Ahead of the Curve?: UN Ideas and Global Challenges*. Bloomington: Indiana University Press, 2001.

Jolly, Richard, et.al. *UN Contributions to Development Thinking and Practice*. Bloomington: Indiana University Press, 2001.

Murphy, Craig N. *The United Nations Development Programme: A Better Way?* New York: Cambridge University Press, 2006.

Singer, Hans, and D. John Shaw. *International Development Co-operation: Essays on Aid and the United Nations System.* Basingstoke, UK: Palgrave, 2001.

Taniguchi, Makoto. *North-South Issues in the 21st Century: A Challenge in the Global Age.* Tokyo: Waseda University Press, 2001.

Toye, John, and Richard Toye. *The UN and Global Political Economy: Trade, Finance, and Development.* Bloomington: Indiana University Press, 2004.

Chapter 6: Rights and responsibilities: human rights to human security

Clapham, Andrew. *Human Rights: A Very Short Introduction.* Oxford: Oxford University Press, 2007.

Dutt, Sagarika. *UNESCO and a Just World Order.* New York: Nova Science Publishers, 2002.

Hunt, Lynn. *Inventing Human Rights: A History.* New York: Norton, 2007.

Loescher, Gil. *The UNHCR and World Politics: A Perilous Path.* New York: Oxford University Press, 2001.

Shaw, D. John, *The UN World Food Programme and the Development of Food Aid.* Basingstoke: Palgrave, 2001.

Steiner, Niklaus. *Problems of Protection: The UNHCR, Refugees and Human Rights.* London: Routledge, 2003.

Thakur, Ramesh. *The United Nations, Peace and Security From Collective Security to the Responsibility to Protect.* New York: Cambridge University Press, 2006.

White, Nigel. *The United Nations System: Toward International Justice.* Boulder, CO: Lynne Rienner, 2002.

Chapter 7: Reform and challenges: the future of the UN

Bowles, Newton. The *Diplomacy of Hope: The United Nations since the Cold War.* New York: I. B. Tauris, 2004.

Muravchik, Joshua. *The Future of the United Nations: Understanding the Past to Chart a Way Forward.* Washington, DC: AEI Press, 2005.

Index

P

Index

Index

Expand your collection of
VERY SHORT INTRODUCTIONS